RANDOM RAMBLINGS:
BEYOND THE EVERYDAY

REFLECTIONS FROM ORDINARY MOMENTS THAT QUIETLY BECOME MEMORIES

KAIZAR TURABALI SHAKIR

Clever Fox® PUBLISHING
Chennai • Bangalore

CLEVER FOX PUBLISHING
Chennai, India

Published by CLEVER FOX PUBLISHING 2026

ISBN: 978-93-7500-661-9

PREFACE

Random Ramblings – Beyond the Everyday is the culmination of reflections gathered over years of observation, introspection, and experience. Most of the reflections in the book began as scribbles in notebooks or fragments saved on my laptop between work, travel, or conversations. Somewhere along the way, these fragments started forming patterns, which were glimpses of how I think, feel, and make sense of the world around us. Over time, they evolved into what is now this collection.

Random Ramblings – Beyond the Everyday looks gently at the fabric of ordinary life - the small moments, the daily contradictions, the quiet lessons that appear when we stop hurrying. These essays trace the soft outlines of human nature: humility, patience, gratitude, confusion, and curiosity - all the things that make us real.

Each piece comes from a specific spark: a conversation that lingered longer than expected, a news story that refused to fade, a passing encounter on the road, or a rule of traffic that turned out to be wiser than it seemed. None of this was meant to be profound, yet the ordinary has a way of teaching if you listen long enough. Meaning hides in familiar corners - you just need to tilt your head slightly to notice it.

This book doesn't hand out conclusions. It asks questions, often softly. It looks at the pauses between words, the humour tucked into routine frustrations, and the subtle ironies that follow us everywhere. These reflections are not about the world out there as much as they are about the one that lives quietly inside us.

My thoughts wander - through ideas, memories, emotions, and contradictions - and they rarely take the shortest route. But perhaps that's the point. These writings wander too, without apology. Some of them may make you smile, others might make you stop for a moment, and a few could nudge you to see things differently. That, I think, is reason enough to write.

This book is also a note of gratitude - to everyone who listened, questioned, encouraged, or disagreed with kindness. What began as a set of scattered thoughts became something more coherent because of them.

While reading, if you find yourself pausing, smiling at a familiar thought or perhaps feeling a note of recognition, then these pages have done what they were meant to. The true wisdom of life lies not in grand revelations, but in small realizations that appear during traffic jams, WhatsApp chats, or casual moments. If this book helps you notice even one of those moments, then Random Ramblings has found its place - somewhere between your thoughts and mine.

ACKNOWLEDGEMENT - THOSE WHO MADE THE WORDS POSSIBLE

To the **Almighty**, the silent Composer of every heartbeat and thought. Whatever I have written is only because He allowed me to feel, to see, and to breathe amidst the beauty of His creation. Every word, every reflection, is borrowed from the life He gifted and the world He crafted.

To my **late grandparents**, whose simplicity was their wealth and whose blessings continue to light my path. They taught me that true grace lies not in what you have, but in how you live.

To my **parents**, for being the reason I exist, and for teaching me that existence itself is not enough unless lived with purpose. For showing me that love needs no language, that values speak louder than words and that humility is the finest inheritance a child can receive. Every achievement of mine carries your invisible fingerprints - unseen, yet always there.

To my **sister**, Tasniem, my pillar of strength who silently holds up the walls when my thoughts wander too far.

To my **brother**, Aliasgar, who reminds me that reasoning is as important as dreaming.

To my **wife**, Jumana, who has edited my moods, managed my chaos, and believed in me even when my words didn't make sense.

And to my **boys**, Mohammed and Hatim, whose idea of what a dad should look like includes a kind heart, patient ears, and a proudly earned belly. I've tried (many times, even bought new shoes for it) to change that image by hitting the gym, but they remind me that dads aren't meant to have abs, they're meant to have stories, smiles, and maybe a little extra space for love and dessert.

To my **school teachers and college professors**, who shaped my mind and showed me that learning never really ends, it just changes classrooms. This book, in a way, is my final exam, written in gratitude, not graded by marks.

To my **friends**, the unsuspecting receivers of my random midnight ramblings and WhatsApp musings. You read, laughed, questioned, and encouraged. Without you, these thoughts would have remained unsent drafts floating in my phone.

And to my **dear friend, M. R. Raghu**, who not only believed but took it upon himself to make this dream tangible. Every book needs an anchor; he was mine.

Lastly, to all those whose names don't find place here but whose presence has always mattered, you know who you are. You were the silent punctuation marks in my story, sometimes a pause, sometimes a full stop, but always a part of the sentence that made sense.

For all of you, and for everything that was, is, and will be - thank you for making my journey worth writing about.

AUTHOR'S NOTE & DISCLAIMER

Before you step into these pages, a small note from me.

Everything you read here comes from moments we all live through - quiet drives, long signals, old memories that suddenly make sense, conversations that stay back in the mind, and the simple truths we often forget in the rush of deadlines and expectations. Some thoughts are shaped by scriptures, books, and wise voices I've crossed paths with over the years. I've made every effort to keep the references authentic and faithful to their sources.

Where I've referred to such works, I've done so with full respect for the original creators. I have no intention whatsoever to violate copyrights, patents, or any protected intellectual property. If any reference has slipped, been quoted loosely, or interpreted differently, it is purely unintentional.

Nothing here is written to misrepresent, offend, or claim expertise over any belief, philosophy, or school of thought. These are reflections - not instructions, not directives, and definitely not professional advice of any kind.

While the experiences, observations, and stories are shared in good faith, any errors, if they exist, are accidental. The author disclaim any liability for actions, decisions, or consequences arising from the use or interpretation of this material.

Read this book the way it is meant to be read - as an honest attempt to make sense of life's everyday chaos, with a smile where possible and with gentleness where needed.

CONTENTS

On Growing Old (Gracefully or Otherwise)

Better to grow old with a sense of humour than with no sense at all. Someone sent me this line today, and just yesterday I was watching A Man Called Otto on Netflix. If you've seen it, you'll know Otto is the perfect example of what happens when age takes away your patience but not your sharp tongue. He is grumpy, snappy, and convinced the world has gone downhill. Yet beneath the frown lies a man with a story, one who eventually finds light in the most unexpected places.

That's the irony of growing old - the years gift you experience, but they also tempt you into bitterness if you let them. You can spend your evenings listing out what's wrong with the neighbour's kids, the government, or the price of onions. Or you can laugh at yourself when you forget why you walked into the kitchen in the first place. (By the way, I've now started calling it "exercise with a purpose.")

I've seen both kinds of people around me. There's the uncle who still walks with a spring in his step, cracking jokes about his cholesterol as if it were a mischievous child he can't discipline. And then there's another who insists on telling everyone how life was better 40 years ago, and how no one today knows how to live, work, or even breathe properly. Guess whose company people enjoy more?

Wisdom may or may not come with age - sometimes age just shows up alone, uninvited, with wrinkles and back pain. But humour? That's a choice. The ability to laugh at your own mistakes, to treat setbacks as stories for tomorrow's dinner table, is what makes life lighter.

And here's another truth: growing old also means knowing when to step aside. Recognition, status, power - they're all nice, but after a while, hanging on to them too tightly just makes you look like the last guest at a wedding who won't leave even though the chairs are being stacked, and the lights are off. There comes a time to give up the driver's seat and let the younger lot take the wheel - preferably before you start confusing the accelerator with the brake!

Think about it: when the elevator breaks down, you can either curse your luck climbing those stairs, or you can call it your free gym membership for the day. When your children "borrow" your things and never return them, you can yell, or you can smile knowing they are carrying pieces of you in their messy rooms. And when the young ones are ready to lead, you can sulk about not being in charge anymore, or you can cheer them on - while enjoying the front-row seat and the freedom to finally order dessert without worrying about office politics.

The truth is, we don't control how long we live, but we do control how we live those years. Grumpy, snobbish, arrogant? That's one route. Humorous, cheerful, contented? That's another. And the funny thing is, the second option not only makes life easier for you but also for everyone who has to deal with you.

So yes, maybe the secret to ageing well is not wisdom in the grand sense, but a pocketful of humour, a pinch of lightness, and the humility to move on. After all, life doesn't stop for anyone. Why should we stop living while we are still alive?

Shades of Grey - Minus the Fifty

Life is never simply black or white. It moves in countless shades of grey - sometimes lighter, sometimes darker, but rarely in absolutes. People who claim to see everything in black and white often forget that situations and circumstances shape our actions. Life isn't a scientific equation; it's art. And art is abstract.

To live meaningfully, one must mould, give in, compromise, and sometimes even succumb. This isn't weakness; it takes far more strength to bend than to stand rigid. Relationships are often more valuable than uprightness. Yet, this does not mean that morals, ethics, and values are for sale. Those remain untouchable. What it does mean is that balance is needed, knowing when to soften and when to stay firm.

I've seen this balance play out in many ways. A father strict with his children on discipline will, as a grandfather, happily spoil his grandchildren. Did his principles vanish? No. Circumstances changed. At work, one manager might stick blindly to "the contract," losing a vendor forever. Another may bend slightly, accommodate a delay, and in return gain trust and loyalty. The latter is no less ethical, just wiser.

Even in friendships, shades of grey show. A harsh word or forgotten moment can strain ties. But if the bond matters, you choose to forgive, not because you are weak, but because love weighs more than pride.

This balance carries into every role we play. With parents, we owe respect; with a spouse, companionship; with children, patience; with friends, honesty; with colleagues, cooperation; with business partners, fairness; with vendors, trust; with customers, reliability; with superiors, loyalty; and with subordinates, encouragement. Each role demands a different response, a different shade of grey.

Life then is an art of balance - standing tall without arrogance, yielding without losing oneself. Grey is not weakness. Grey is the wisdom of experience

When Life gives Tangerines

Yesterday, over a simple cup of coffee with a friend, what began as lighthearted reminiscing slowly turned into something deeper. He spoke about life's unexpected turns and experiences that had left their mark on him. And then, almost as if he was revealing a truth, he himself had carried for long, he quoted a close friend of his:

"Just because you're a good person, doesn't mean the world owes you kindness."

That line struck me. It lingers even now.

We grow up believing that good deeds will automatically bring good fortune, that fairness will be repaid with fairness, and kindness will echo back in equal measure. But life doesn't always work like a neat equation. The world is not bound by a contract to treat us well simply because we chose to walk the path of goodness.

The true value of being good is not in the applause it brings, but in the quiet strength it builds within us. It's about staying true to our principles even when circumstances push us otherwise. Kindness may not always return from the same place you give it, but it does return, often in unexpected ways.

And so, when life gives you lemons, you make lemonade. When life gives you tangerines, you don't just eat them - you turn them into marmalade. In other words, whatever comes your way, sweet or sour, use it to create something of value.

Being good, then, is not a bargain with the world. It's a commitment to yourself. A way of saying, "No matter what comes my way, I won't let bitterness define me." The reward is not always in what we receive, but in the peace of knowing we didn't lose ourselves along the way.

So perhaps the point is not to expect kindness in exchange, but to be kind regardless. Life may not always play fair, but in choosing to stay good, we ensure that at least we do. And that, in itself, is a quiet victory

The Logic Behind the Ordinary

Why is a dozen twelve? Because twelve divides so neatly by two, three, four, and six. Traders found it convenient, the French gave it structure, and since then the world has bought eggs, bread, and buns by the dozen without question. We never pause to ask why twelve? And yet, when you think about it, isn't life also easier when we learn to divide? Dividing time, work, worries, and even responsibilities make burdens lighter. The dozen reminds us that simplicity lies not in having less, but in knowing how to share and arrange.

Why is red for stop and green for go? Red is the loudest colour to the human eye, impossible to ignore. Green is calm, safe, and reassuring. Over time, the world accepted this as a rule of the road. But here lies a thought: what if we too could learn to "see red" when we must pause? Not out of fear, but out of wisdom. And what if we recognised the "green" moments of our lives, moving forward when it is safe, not rushing blindly? The colours teach us that life has its signals; we just need to notice them.

Why is the wedding ring worn on the fourth finger? Long ago, people believed a vein in that finger led directly to the heart. Science has long disproved it, but the romance remains. The tradition teaches us something important: sometimes the truth is less about facts and more about meaning. Not everything we do needs the stamp of logic; some things we carry forward simply because they make life beautiful. Love, after all, is less about reason and more about faith.

Why do we shake hands? Once, it was to show you carried no weapon - palm open, arm extended, a gesture of peace. Today it is a greeting, a seal of trust. But here is the deeper lesson: in life, every handshake is not just skin touching skin, it is a silent promise. A promise that "I come to you in peace, I come to you without harm." Imagine if every relationship, personal or professional, carried the same honesty as that original handshake. How much better would our world be?

All these customs began with reason, with belief, with practicality. Over centuries, the "why" was forgotten, and only the act remained. We follow without asking. And maybe that is where we lose something essential. For the moment we stop questioning, our thirst for understanding begins to dry up.

The dozen is not just about numbers, the red light not just about traffic, the ring not just about tradition, the handshake not just about etiquette. Each whispers a lesson, waiting for us to listen. The ordinary holds meaning, if we dare to ask.

So let curiosity never die. Let us not live like passengers on a bus, staring blankly out of the window. Let us live like wanderers on a journey, pausing, asking, wondering. Because it is only when we question that we quench the thirst of curiosity and in that quenching, we truly begin to live

Inked Memories

Life's journey can be traced in the story of a pen. We speak not of reed pens or quill pens, but of the pens I grew up with.

In kindergarten and the early school years, it was all about pencils - constantly sharpening, erasing, and carrying that small sense of responsibility to keep them neat. Grades 5 to 7 brought the big leap to fountain pens. Ink bottles, fillers, spare nibs - suddenly we were no longer kids. That proud smudge of blue on the side of the middle finger was a mark of growing up. I still remember my first Parker, gifted by my grandfather, while Hero pens were the most popular among us. Some fancy ones carried Cross, Waterman or Sheaffer, but most of us bought the sturdy local pens from the corner stationery shop.

By grade 8, ballpoint pens entered the scene. Reynolds 045 was everywhere, BiC became a craze, and my cousins swore by their Lamy pens. Soon came the Cello Gripper and Linc, which felt so smooth. Then Rotomac stormed in with its unforgettable line , "likhte hi likhte jao". College added another phase: friends gifted me Pilot Hi-Techpoint and Uniball pens, introducing me to use-and-throw luxury. Exams, notes, and assignments flowed through these very pens, each brand a chapter in memory.

Later, as I began working, I dreamt of Montblancs but couldn't afford one. My mother, knowing my quiet desire, surprised me with not one but two; an engraved fountain pen and a fine liner. The joy was unmatched. Over the years, I added a few more - Montblanc, Dupont (a gift), Waterman - but even today, I often use a simple KD 1-a-dozen pen that writes beautifully and causes no worry if lost.

Looking back, pens were not just tools. They shaped my handwriting, my patience, and even the rhythm of my thoughts. A fountain pen slowed me down, a ballpoint gave me speed, a fine tip demanded neatness. Each phase of pen taught me something - not just about writing, but about life.

Now, with keyboards and touchscreens ruling, our three fingers that once gripped the pen are reduced to two thumbs and two fingertips. Yet, I still believe the pen must remain. It is not only mightier than the sword; it is also gentler than a screen. Writing by hand creates a bond between thought and paper that typing cannot.

So, my message to all - read to stimulate the mind but also write to keep your fingers and thoughts alive. Don't just sign documents. Scribble, jot, and write for the joy of it. Because every pen we hold is not just ink and plastic - it is a witness to our growing up, our learning, and our becoming. A pen doesn't just write words; it writes the person holding it

If

Today I was thinking about Kipling's poem If. I first read it in school, tucked away at the back of an English textbook. At that time, it was just a poem to memorize, one more lesson before the exam. But as years passed, I began to see that it was not just about words, it was about life itself.

"If you can keep your head when all about you

Are losing theirs and blaming it on you…"

Those lines came alive for me during my Sea Cadet Corps days. On the parade ground, standing in uniform, one small mistake could bring anger from seniors. The real lesson was not in the drill, but in keeping calm when everyone else lost theirs.

I still remember hosting a quiz in college. I fumbled, forgot my line, and thought I had ruined it all. Yet the applause that followed told me something else - mistakes do not end us. They only remind us to stand again.

For Chartered Accountants too, this poem speaks louder than any textbook. Not everyone clears in the first attempt. Some try again and again, each failure heavier than the last. But then come the lines that carry us through:

*"If you can force your heart and nerve and sinew
To serve your turn long after they are gone,
And so, hold on when there is nothing in you
Except the Will which says to them: 'Hold on!'"
That is the real meaning of perseverance.
Another part of the poem that impressed me on humility:

"If you can talk with crowds and keep your virtue,
Or walk with Kings - nor lose the common touch,
If neither foes nor loving friends can hurt you,
If all men count with you, but none too much;"

These lines remind me of the balance life constantly asks of us. To achieve yet not become arrogant. To have influence yet never lose the ability to sit on the floor with ordinary people. To accept praise without pride, and criticism without bitterness. I have seen this in the simplest of people - teachers who guided us with patience, seniors who treated juniors with respect, parents who sacrificed without seeking recognition.

And as I thought about it, another realization struck me; every day is just the same twenty-four hours, the same sun rising and setting. Yet we call it a worst day, a bad day, a good day, or a best day. The day itself does not change. It is our situation, our mood, our circumstances that give it those adjectives. What feels like the worst day today may become the day that shaped us most.

So, my rambling today is simple: never give up, never stop trying, never think a bad day defines your life. Keep going. Some days will test you; some will reward you; some will break you; and some will lift you. But all days pass. What matters is that you keep moving forward.

And perhaps then, Kipling's last line will always ring true in our hearts:

"...you'll be a Man, my son!"

The Blessings of Being Human

News came of Judge Frank Caprio's passing - the man from Caught in Providence whose courtroom was not just a place of judgment, but a place of kindness, forgiveness, and humanity. He reminded the world that the law may be blind, but justice must never be deaf to compassion.

His life was a reminder of something we often forget in the rush of authority, power, and position - that humility is not weakness, and compassion is not a compromise. A smile, a kind word, an understanding ear, or even a gentle laugh shared with someone standing on the edge of despair can sometimes carry more weight than the strictest rule book.

People like Judge Caprio show us that you don't need to touch millions directly. Touch a few with sincerity, and those few will carry it forward. That ripple grows into waves far beyond what you can see. This is a lesson for autocrats and dictators, for technocrats and bureaucrats, for jurists, politicians, and corporate leaders - that the real measure of influence is not in how much fear you command, but how much respect you earn through humanity.

Humility is about being approachable. Simplicity is about remembering that everyone before you is, first and foremost, a human being. When someone comes to you for help, for guidance, for support, don't see it as a burden of your position. See it as a blessing that the Almighty chose you to be the one at that moment. Not everyone gets that chance. To be in a position where you can change even one life is not a privilege to boast about, it is a responsibility to be grateful for.

I often repeat my grandfather's words: "Namey te sav ne gamey." For those who don't understand Gujarati, it means - the one who is humble is liked by all. It is a simple truth that carries the weight of ages.

So, in remembering Judge Caprio, let us remember that being human is the highest honour. The rest - titles, designations, authority are temporary. What remains is whether you were kind, whether you were just, and whether you carried your blessings with gratitude

Shades of Grey and the Gift of Perspective

Count your blessings. Some people find it difficult to do that. They carry a habit of cribbing and complaining, of beginning every conversation with a "no" or a "why." No matter the situation, they manage to find something wrong in people, in projects, in authorities, in governments. It's as if satisfaction is an unfamiliar feeling to them.

I often feel like telling them, try looking at the brighter side. Be positive. My blood group, by coincidence, is B Positive, and perhaps that's a small reminder in itself. I believe everything happens for a reason, even when the reason is hidden from us. We may think we know it all, just as Moses (PBUH) once thought, until God introduced him to Khidr, who showed him that what we see is only part of a much larger story.

That is why I try to remain a student in life; positive, humble, and modest. It's important to pause and understand another person's perspective. The world is not just black or white; it is filled with shades of grey. Policies, procedures, and laws are created to bring order, and as long as they remain within the boundaries of the constitution, they deserve respect.

But respect does not mean blind acceptance. It means thinking with clarity, applying sound judgement, and keeping a balanced view. It means not leaning to one side out of habit or bias but being willing to see things as they truly are, even if that means challenging our own certainty.

In the end, wisdom is not in winning every argument, but in realising that the truth is often bigger than our vision. And sometimes, being right matters less than being kind.

Step Back, Breathe - Things We Will See When We Slow Down

There are days when I feel the world is spinning a bit too fast. Too loud. Too reckless. Everyone seems to be in a hurry - to achieve, to win, to prove, to conquer; and somewhere in this mad rush, we've forgotten the essence of just being. Not achieving, not acquiring, not asserting. Just... being.

World leaders are constantly chanting slogans of greatness. "Make this great again, make that better than before." But do they ever pause to ask: at what cost? Are they truly leading their countries forward, or merely dragging them through their own self-serving agendas wrapped in the cloak of nationalism and legacy? In the process, societies are torn apart, unity is shattered, and hate is legitimised, all for the throne of momentary relevance.

Educators and policymakers - they too need to take a step back. What are we teaching? What kind of youth are we grooming? Are we building free thinkers or obedient followers boxed into ideologies? Are our policies liberating or are they creating boundaries so narrow that creativity and common sense don't even find a corner to breathe?

Corporate heads, CEOs, boardrooms full of suits - all talking big about ESG, sustainability, AI driven growth, stakeholder capitalism. But is it really development? Or just another race in fancy packaging to dominate and outdo competition, exploit loopholes, and shine on glossy annual reports? We see economic wars being fought every day, without much economic development to show for it.

And then there are the ones who write, debate, influence - media moguls, social commentators, celebrity voices. All needing to pause too. Are they really informing and inspiring, or just feeding the chaos for clicks, likes and TRPs?

Even the judiciary, the spiritual leaders, the ones considered to be society's conscience - they're not untouched by noise. Somewhere, justice is not blind, it's blinkered. Faith has turned to fear-mongering. And people follow either helplessly or hopelessly.

We live in a world of visa bans, protests, travel uncertainties, hate crimes, school shootings, fabricated narratives and silenced truths. And still, the daily routine carries on like a conveyor belt. Emails. Meetings. Sale targets. Appraisals. Strategic plans.

A few days ago, I felt the emptiness of my family leaving again. The sudden silence. I even wrote about the 'empty nest.' But just like that, work resumed, responsibilities piled up, and that emotion got tucked away somewhere. We bounce back so fast, don't we?

Just like when we attend a funeral, be it of a loved one or a respected elder. The philosophical chat begins: this is the end, this is life's reality, the kings and the beggars all lie side by side. Nothing comes with us. All this hoarding and hustling, what for? But as we walk out of the crematorium or cemetery, we get back into our cars and back to our calendars. The next call, the next deal, the next deadline.

Maybe God made human memory a short-term phenomenon for a reason. Imagine holding on to every loss, every high, every heartbreak, every tear or burst of joy. We'd be paralysed in the past, unable to live the present. This forgetfulness is both a curse and a gift. It helps us move on. Maybe too quickly.

And yet, what strikes me most is how this cycle doesn't seem to touch those in positions of power. They don't pause. They don't reflect. They are too seasoned, too strategic. It's almost like empathy and accountability have been filtered out of their systems. Manipulation, spin, and self-interest have taken their place.

Somehow, the interest of the common man, the community, the country, that sacred trust lies abandoned on the lowest step of their ladder to personal glory.

Maybe, just maybe, we all need to step back. Breathe. Re-align. Life's not waiting. But we can choose to slow down. Even if for a bit.

Even if just for today

Somewhere Between Zero and Infinity

One of the most interesting things I've read recently wasn't from a financial journal or an inspirational novel but a WhatsApp message, in one of our groups, of a story shared by a student about his old Mechanics professor at IIT. The kind of anecdote that quietly stays with you and pops back in the middle of the daily noise.

The professor had a way of teaching that didn't just stick to textbooks. He asked the class one day: "How do you know you are rich?"

Before the class could dive into discussions of net worth, assets, bank balances, or big salaries, he introduced a different lens. A lens of wants and income. He said: If your wants are more than your income, you are poor. If your wants are less than your income, you are rich. Simple. Uncomfortable. Honest. But then he went a step further - he connected this idea to Zero and Infinity

He asked three questions:

1. What is Zero?
2. What is Infinity?
3. Can Zero and Infinity ever be the same?

The class had textbook answers ready:

Zero means nothing. Infinity means a number larger than anything countable. And obviously, they can't be the same.

But the professor, like all good teachers, knew the magic lay in making you think differently.

He explained that for someone who can count only up to twenty - say, a shepherd who's never learned numbers beyond that - anything beyond that is simply "too many." That's his infinity. Similarly, for someone comparing the size of the Earth to the distance from Earth to the Sun, the Earth is "too small." Practically zero.

Zero, then, isn't nothing. It's too little. Infinity isn't some mythical number. It's too much. Same object, different scale, different outcome. What's zero to one can be infinite to another.

That's when it hits you. The relationship between poverty and richness is like the relationship between zero and infinity. It all depends on your scale. Your frame of comparison.

In our everyday life, we don't always get to control our income. Not everyone gets a bonus. Not every pitch closes. Not every effort result in growth. But we do have some control over our wants. And sometimes, even reducing one or two can make life feel a bit lighter.

What's even more interesting is that this professor's lesson isn't really about money at all. It's about contentment. A man with few wants and limited income can sleep peacefully. A man with everything but an ever-growing appetite might never find rest.

I've come to think - richness isn't a state you arrive at with a fat wallet. It's a space you enter when your needs stop chasing your dreams, and your wants stop bullying your peace. Somewhere between zero and infinity, there's a point where you feel full. You're not poor because you have little. You're not rich because you have a lot. You're rich because you need less.

And that, to me, is the quietest form of wealth

When Life Skips Your Scoop - The Pinkberry Lesson

Yesterday was a Pinkberry day at home. Sitting comfortably with a tub in my hand, I scooped out a spoon and offered it behind me. Both my nieces - my sister's daughter and my brother's daughter - opened their mouths in perfect synchrony, like little hungry birds.

I gave it to my brother's daughter.

Second scoop. Again, both opened their mouths. Again, I fed my brother's daughter.

Third scoop. Both opened their mouths. This time, I didn't feed anyone.

Fourth scoop. Same suspense. No feeding.

My sister's daughter, visibly upset, said, "Katti!" - meaning she wouldn't talk to me.

I smiled and said, "It's okay… don't talk."

Honestly, I was tempted to give her a motivational life lesson right there on expectation, rejection, patience, and strategy… but I abstained.

Today evening, she reminded me. "I'm still not talking to you."

I smiled again. Gave her a small pep talk on how life doesn't always give us what we expect, when we expect it, just because we open our mouth or think we deserve it.

She looked at me, eyes wide, and said, "Why do you always have an answer for everything? How do you turn tables like that?"

I told her I'd write my justifications in my diary today.

She insisted she would approve them before I publish. But well... here I am... writing them anyway.

Because, in life, expectations are like scoops of Pinkberry. The more you sit expecting it to come into your mouth, the more disappointed you'll be when it doesn't. Sometimes, you've got to pick up your own spoon, get up, and scoop it yourself.

And yes - don't let negative thoughts swirl in just because someone didn't do what you wanted them to. People have their own reasons. Ice cream melts, life moves on, and so should we.

Lesson of the day: If life doesn't feed you the Pinkberry scoop you're waiting for... remember, it's probably because it wants you to burn a few calories first and sometimes the spoon skips you, not because you don't deserve it, but because life wants to check how dramatic your "katti" face can get

The Bedspread Realisation

Last Saturday, we visited a reputed home store - the kind where the lighting is warm, the displays are poetic, and every bed looks like it belongs to someone who meditates at sunrise and never spills chai.

After some deliberation (and silent prayers to the budget gods), we bought a duvet cover described as "neutral-toned with rich texture and effortless elegance." On display, under that amber showroom lighting, it looked like luxury itself - calm, composed, and perfectly creased.

But at home, under our own warm lights - the lived-in kind - the same duvet looked... confused.

The "taupe" suddenly leaned into a shade I can only describe as Sunday morning. The texture now felt like an overenthusiastic linen shirt. And the effortless elegance? Well, we were definitely making an effort.

We tried adjusting the pillows, shifting the angle, dimming the lights - even squinting a bit. But the truth was visible: beautiful things in stores don't always translate to beautiful things in our lives.

So, we folded it back - not quite as artistically as it was displayed - and returned it.

And somewhere in that act, a quiet lesson emerged.

In life too, many things look perfect under the glow of presentation - choices, jobs, even people. But true comfort is only found when something fits into your space, your rhythm, your version of home.

There's no shame in realising something doesn't fit. Only wisdom in gently letting it go.

Even the finest bedspread is only worth keeping... if you can actually sleep peacefully under it. No hard feelings, only soft lessons

"The Warmth That Truly Matters"

There's a kind of warmth that has nothing to do with temperature. Not the 46 degrees we were discussing today with the school Principal, wondering how hot it might get by peak summer. That's heat. What I'm talking about is something else. Something quieter, deeper, and far more lasting.

I was invited for an expert talk at a school today. A simple event on the surface. But the real value wasn't in the mic or the message-it was in the moments. The Director, whom I hadn't met in nearly two decades, greeted me with a smile that skipped the years in between. The Principal and the faculty didn't just offer hospitality-they offered connection. Their words, their gestures, their eyes-all warm. That's the kind of warmth I'm referring to.

You feel it in childhood. In your mother's palm on your forehead when you're unwell. In your father's silent presence during a difficult day. In a tiffin that always had your favourite snack, without you having to ask.

In school, it's the friend who shares their answer sheet under the desk. Or the one who walks home with you in silence after a bad grade. Not trying to fix things-just being there.

In your youth, warmth shows up as a mentor who believes in you more than you do in yourself. Or a colleague who stays late to help, without making a big deal out of it.

And as life moves forward, you begin to realise that warmth has little to do with words, and everything to do with presence.

A simple touch on the shoulder, a cup of chai brought unasked, a message from someone saying, "Just checking in."

Even at work-where charts and KPIs rule-there are moments. Someone says "take your time" when you're clearly flustered. Or they remember that your son had an exam yesterday and ask how it went. It's in the details, not the drama.

And in old age, warmth is no longer an add-on-it becomes everything. You remember fewer names but more feelings. The neighbour who checks on you. The grandchild who runs into your arms like you're their whole world. The friend who just sits with you, saying nothing, needing nothing.

In our talk today, while we were wondering about the unbearable summer heat, I smiled to myself-because the warmth I carried home wasn't from the sun or the weather app. It came from people. From genuine conversation. From eyes that smiled before lips did.

In a world that's often rushed, loud, and digital, warmth is the quiet rebel. It doesn't demand attention-but once felt, it's never forgotten.

Let's be the reason someone feels it today.

Warmly,

Still choosing warmth overheat, every time

The Other Side of The Story

This one is a blend of a couple of thoughts I've written before - on perspective, on the habit of wanting to please, and on how we judge ourselves and others.

There's that old line I often come back to: you can please some people all the time and all people some of the time, but pleasing everyone all the time is a dream best left alone. Even when intentions are clean and actions are fair, reactions vary. People see the same moment through different windows.

A lot of it comes from the little storms we all carry inside - envy, insecurity, ego, pride, or just a different expectation. We tend to hold a generous view of ourselves but a critical one of others. That's why even without full information, assumptions take flight. Living rooms turn into debate clubs, half-truths grow wings, and opinions form faster than facts.

Across faiths, the message has always been the same.

The Bhagavad Gita cautions against actions coloured by ego.

The Quran discourages backbiting and suspicion.

The Bible reminds us not to judge in haste.

Different voices, one lesson - be mindful of what you speak and why you speak it.

Expectations also play their role. Sometimes someone feels a greeting could have been warmer. Sometimes someone assumes they were taken for granted. No one wrong, no one right, just two angles that missed meeting.

Life is too short for bruised egos, stretched misunderstandings, and silent resentments.

Too short for reading too much into small moments. Too short for holding ourselves too high and others too low.

Letting go helps. Seeing from the other side helps. Understanding before reacting helps. And keeping the ego quiet helps even more.

At the end of the day, it's easier to be your own selfie - clear, honest, unfiltered. If your conscience is clean, let the chatter die on its own. Those who truly matter will speak to you, not about you. And those who value perspective will always choose understanding over assumption.

A simple reminder to keep moving with grace

Facing It

Not everything that is faced in life can be changed. But nothing can be changed until it is faced.

How true. We often spend half our lives trying to avoid the very things that need our attention. Problems, people, emotions, or decisions. We push them under the carpet hoping they'll somehow disappear. But carpets have a strange way of tripping us later.

In our professional lives, especially as leaders, we face hundreds of things we can't control - market shifts, client moods, policy changes. But what we can control is our willingness to confront them. The moment we face reality as it is, not as we wish it to be, we gain the power to respond wisely.

In life too, it's the same. Whether it's a health concern, a strained relationship, or a career doubt - the longer we delay, the heavier it gets. Facing it doesn't mean we'll always fix it. But it means we stop running. And that's half the battle won.

I had a friend once with whom things went sour over a small misunderstanding. We stopped speaking - no confrontation, no closure, just silence. Months passed. Then, one evening, he showed up unannounced. No long explanations, just a casual "Let's put this behind us." That's all it took. The moment he faced it, everything softened. Pride melted, and friendship quietly returned. Looking back, I realized it could've been me too who made that call. But it was his courage that saved something valuable.

Then there was the car incident - just six months ago, near my office. Someone hit my parked car and drove away. I didn't think much could come of it, but the security cameras caught his number plate, and he was eventually traced. When he came to see me, he was visibly scared, expecting anger or a report. I simply told him, "It's fine. Next time, just face it. It's easier." He was surprised - almost relieved. Funny enough, he now messages me every few weeks asking if I know of any job openings! Life does have a sense of humour.

I think that's the essence of facing things - it changes both people. The one who faces grows braver, and the one who forgives grows lighter. In the end, it's not about being right or wrong. It's about being real.

Whether it's a strained friendship, a mistake, or a moment of fear - once you face it, life moves. Maybe not perfectly, but it moves. And that's all we really need - movement, not escape

So, whatever stands in front of you today, don't look away. Face it. It might not change everything, but it will surely change you

CHAPTER 2

SOCIETY, LEADERSHIP & POWER

Power, Politics, and the Price of Corruption

Power, politics, position, privilege, property, profit, and propaganda - each of these "P's" seems to circle around corruption like moths around a flame. The deeper one looks into the functioning of governments, corporates, or institutions of faith, the more one realizes how contaminated the system is.

Take politicians first. Those who rise to authority rarely get there by virtue of knowledge or integrity. More often, it is manipulation, influence, nepotism, and an ability to bend rules that carry them forward. Billionaires emerge from nowhere. The same leaders who claim to serve the people somehow multiply their fortunes through family members, shell companies, and ingenious channels that cannot be easily traced. Nepotism is so deeply ingrained that family trees often become political dynasties, where power is handed down like inheritance. Their speeches may drip with patriotism, but their actions reveal a hunger for personal gain, often at the cost of the poor and the voiceless.

Then there are the clergy, religious heads, and self-styled spiritual guides. The hypocrisy here is glaring. Their mantra seems to be: don't do what I do, do what I say. While their words preach morality, sacrifice, and service, their lives reek of privilege, indulgence, and manipulation. Religious and spiritual institutions thrive as businesses, where "heaven" is the product on sale, and no one has ever come back to demand a refund. Exploitation takes refined forms - whether it is blind faith, emotional manipulation, or subtle slavery disguised as service.

Corporates, too, walk the same road. They cloak themselves in words like "innovation," "sustainability," and "social responsibility," but behind the curtain lie profit-driven agendas, manipulative monopolies, and financial gymnastics that rival the tricks of politicians. For every genuine entrepreneur building with integrity, there are countless conglomerates bending laws, funding campaigns, and influencing policies to protect their empires. Employees often become mere cogs, consumers become statistics, and the shareholders' wealth becomes the supreme god. It is a boardroom version of the same corruption seen in politics and religion - polished, sophisticated, and global.

Even democracy, which was once celebrated as the answer, has turned questionable. In practice, it often turns worse than communism, and communism in turn has at times put autocrats to shame. Dictators and monarchs ruled alone, or as one family. But in modern democracies, hundreds of kin and cronies believe they are privileged to abuse power, bleed the system, and suffocate ordinary citizens. No wonder people rise in revolt. Nepal saw it, Sri Lanka witnessed it, Libya burned in it, and other nations too have toppled their so-called leaders when the exploitation became unbearable. The question remains: does the world need such riots and revolutions every now and then to cleanse the rot?

The irony is that corruption is not limited by geography. It thrives in Asia, Africa, and beyond - a universal disease dressed in different attires. Perhaps the antidote is not knowledge alone. Knowledge humbles, but it is conscience that guides, and compassion that restrains. Knowledge teaches the purpose of life, conscience ensures we act in line with it, and compassion reminds us that power means little if it does not serve others.

In the end, the difference is stark: power enslaves, knowledge liberates; power corrupts, conscience corrects; power feeds ego, compassion nurtures humility.

And so the question remains: do we want to be ruled by power, or guided by knowledge, conscience, and compassion?

The Paradox of Democracy – When Power Outpaces Competence

In the grand theatre of democracy, power flows from the people. And rightly so. It is the people who elect their representatives, entrusting them with the reins of governance. Yet, as I sit back and reflect, I find myself caught in a paradox - where those elected to frame the laws are often less qualified, less experienced, and sometimes even facing criminal charges, while those who interpret and uphold these very laws - the judiciary - are scholars, experts, and stalwarts in their domain.

Is this the irony of modern democracy?

The legislature, in principle, is supreme in a democracy - a reflection of the people's mandate. But does supremacy imply infallibility? When members of parliament carry with them baggage of criminal records and questionable educational credentials, and yet hold the pen that drafts the law, one wonders - are we safeguarding democracy, or diluting it?

On the other side stands the judiciary - bound not by electoral politics, but by the Constitution, by precedent, and by principle. They are not perfect, but they are often better equipped - academically, intellectually, and ethically - to deliberate on complex constitutional questions. Still, they are expected to remain subservient to the will of the people, expressed through those very elected representatives. That's the paradox.

This contradiction reminds me of the plight of our civil servants - and other technocrats - often highly educated, rigorously trained, and yet required to serve under ministers whose grasp on policy, governance, and even basic administration may be tenuous at best. Power outruns knowledge. Influence trumps insight.

I firmly believe that democracy thrives not just on representation, but on qualified representation. Why do we not expect our lawmakers to have a foundational education in law, governance, or public administration? Why do we normalize a situation where a ship is steered by someone who's never learnt to sail?

The essence of democracy lies in inclusivity - yes. But it also lies in accountability, education, integrity, and vision. A democratic nation must not just empower its people to vote, but also to choose wisely. It must create filters where competence and character matter as much as popularity and rhetoric.

The balance between the legislature and the judiciary must be one of mutual respect - not submission. Neither must overstep its role. The judiciary must not legislate, and the legislature must not undermine the judiciary. But for that equilibrium to exist, we must first fix the broken pipeline - we need lawmakers who are worthy of the task.

This note is not aimed at any one nation or continent. It is a generic observation - a reflection on a pattern visible across democracies around the world. Democracy is not just a system. It's a responsibility. When leaders focus on the betterment of all citizens - not just sections, not just vote banks - only then can we say the system is working.

Until then, we remain in a strange paradox - where the architects of law are often less qualified than the interpreters, and where the ones with knowledge serve at the mercy of those with numbers.

My take? Democracy needs an upgrade - not in structure, but in the quality of its stewards

Leadership, Governance, and the Weight of Power

Some nights, the news feels heavier than the day's work. Countries once known for peace now echo with protests. Economies that once boomed now tremble under inflation. And leaders-elected with hopes high-either rise like tall trees or fall, dragging their nations with them.

Leadership is no longer about titles or flags or thumping podiums. It's about what a country wakes up to. It's about whether a child in a village gets clean water, whether a young graduate finds work, whether a widow can sleep without fear. That's the true test-not global headlines, but the daily lives of ordinary people.

Governance is not magic. It's about systems. About running a country like it's owned by the people-not a throne to sit on but a chair that rotates with accountability. A good leader doesn't need to be loved or feared. They just need to be fair. Fair in laws, in taxes, in trade, and in the way they speak to their people.

Economic decisions have a chain reaction. Tax fairly and the state grows. Spend wisely and the economy breathes. Bargain hard on trade, but never at the cost of dignity. Share the nation's wealth not equally-but equitably. It's not about making everyone rich, but about not letting anyone be invisible.

Cross-border trade must be encouraged-not blocked by unnecessary ego or red tape. Medical and educational tourism can bring knowledge, healing, and income, but only if countries work with trust and treat foreigners with respect. And when someone migrates legally, chasing the dream of greener pastures, it is not just a legal entry-it's a transfer of hope. That hope must not be crushed by retroactive laws or shifting policies. It's not fair to build a bridge and then destroy it after people have crossed. People uproot their lives and put faith in the systems of nations. That trust is fragile. Enact laws looking ahead-not backwards. Progress lies in forward movement, not punishing people for yesterday's rules. And while borders exist, humanity must not stop at them.

Don't make people fight in the name of religion, caste, colour, nationality, or gender. These are human-made divisions. The moment leaders begin drawing lines between people instead of connecting them, decay sets in. History is a sharp judge. It remembers those who put their people first, and it never forgets those who ruled for themselves. Some leaders wrote history books worth reading. Others are remembered in footnotes and failures.

Charisma fades. Propaganda dies. But real work stands. Schools built, hospitals maintained, corruption tackled, borders respected, neighbours treated with kindness-that's the stuff that lasts.

Right now, the world's on edge. Too many masks, too many speeches, not enough listening. Global friendships strained, national conversations angry, and the common man always paying the price.

There's a silent hope in every country-that someone somewhere will choose integrity over image. Will choose service over slogans. And will lead without wanting a statue in their name.

And for the believers-if there is a hereafter, surely leadership will be questioned there too. The people's pain will not be forgotten. Those in power must ask themselves: will their deeds stand the test of time-and judgment? Or will they crumble under the weight of what they failed to do?

That, perhaps, is the only leadership worth remembering.

On Leadership

"A leader must have a large heart and broad shoulders."

Someone said this to me over a casual conversation the other day. Not in a boardroom, not in a speech. Just a simple thought dropped mid-sentence - but it stayed with me.

What a beautiful definition. Large heart - to understand, to empathize, to forgive. Broad shoulders - to take responsibility, to protect, to carry the load when others can't.

It made me reflect on how often we confuse leadership with authority. A position, a title, a seat at the head of the table. But true leadership, I've come to realise, isn't always official. It's often unspoken. It happens quietly.

There are people around us - in homes, at work, even in friend circles - who don't carry designations, but everyone instinctively turns to them in a crisis. They don't need a mic; their words are few but weighty. Their calm becomes the compass when everything seems off track.

Not long ago, in a professional setting, there was a moment when decisions had to be made quickly. While others debated and hesitated, one person, without waiting for a formal nod, stepped up. They asked the right questions, involved the right people, and nudged the team forward. There was no drama, no "I'm in charge" declaration. Just an ease with responsibility, and a confidence that comes from clarity, not ego.

What struck me most wasn't the action - it was how natural it seemed. That's what separates leaders from the rest: their ability to do what's needed, not for applause, but because it must be done.

In families too, it's often the ones sitting in the background, listening more than speaking, who become the anchors. They hold the space. They offer wisdom without forcing it. They are not elected but accepted.

Even on the world stage, when you observe moments of crisis - it's never the loudest voice that leads. It's the calmest. The one who doesn't seek credit but offers clarity. The one who doesn't rush to speak but listens first. That pause, that patience - it makes all the difference.

Leadership, I've realised, is not about being followed. It's about being trusted.

It's not about being right all the time. It's about being willing to be wrong - and still show up.

So yes, the next time someone asks me what leadership means, I'll say: it's about having a heart big enough to include others, and shoulders strong enough to carry them when needed. No badge required.

Sometimes, that leader is right beside you. Sometimes, it's you - when you least expect it

The Burden of Power

Power is a strange thing. It can inspire, uplift, and transform nations. But in the wrong hands-or even in the hands of those who start with noble intentions-it can corrupt, divide, and destroy. From the time of Cain and Abel, mankind has been locked in an endless cycle of power struggles, betrayals, and bloodshed. And today, despite all our progress, we see the same patterns repeating on the global stage.

Leaders, whether democratically elected, self-imposed, monarchs, or anarchists, all seem to operate by a single principle: interest. They build alliances not on values but on convenience. They switch sides not out of conviction but out of necessity. The idea of morality, ethics, and responsibility is often just a façade, a carefully crafted illusion that crumbles the moment power is at stake.

We live in a world where the most powerful leaders sit at the center stage-presidents, prime ministers, kings, dictators, and global influencers-making decisions that affect billions. These are people with the power to end wars, to stop hunger, to unite nations. And yet, night after night, they sleep peacefully while thousands die because of their policies, while families are displaced, while children grow up as orphans of war.

How do they sleep? How do they wake up every morning, knowing their hands are stained with decisions that led to suffering? How does their conscience not scream at them? Or have they numbed themselves to the reality of their actions?

What makes it worse is the recklessness with which they speak. Irresponsible statements, thoughtless words, threats, and provocations-often for nothing more than political gain or personal ego-fuel hatred and divisions across the world. They play to their audience, knowing that their words will stir emotions, deepen divides, and spark chaos. They do not speak for humanity. They speak for votes, for power, for influence.

This is not just about politics; it's about humanity. Leadership should be more than strategy and survival. It should be about responsibility, about making the world a better place. Leaders should be role models, good Samaritans, guardians of peace and justice. They should see the world as one, not as a map of territories to be controlled and exploited. They should uplift, not divide. They should bring people together, not push them apart.

But is this just wishful thinking? The history of mankind suggests otherwise. Every era has seen wars, massacres, displacement, and suffering. Religion was meant to guide humanity, yet even faith has been manipulated to serve power. The saffron, green, white, and black robes of clergies preach peace, but their words are often drowned in the noise of politics, greed, and ambition. Morality is not followed-it is twisted and used as a weapon when convenient.

The world burns, and those in power watch, often fueling the fire when it suits them. Will it ever change? Or will the struggle for power, from the first man to the last, continue to define our existence?

Of Czars, Revolutions, and Governance

We are visiting Russia, and it has been a great trip so far. The country has surprised us in the best ways-rich in history, stunning in architecture, and warm in hospitality. Walking through its streets, you don't just see monuments; you feel the echoes of history whispering through them. The grandeur of the czars, the weight of revolutions, the rise and fall of ideologies-it all makes you reflect on the nature of governance and power.

Russia, perhaps more than any other nation, has lived through the extremes of governance. From the absolute rule of the czars to the sweeping tides of the Bolshevik Revolution, from the iron grip of communism to the complex realities of today's state-driven capitalism, it has seen the best and worst of each system. Communism promised equality but delivered control. The Soviet Union was built on the ideals of a classless society, yet, in reality, it bred a new elite-the party leaders, the bureaucrats, the privileged few. The collapse of the USSR was not just an economic failure but a reminder that any system, no matter how idealistic, crumbles when power is centralized without accountability.

Having traveled to monarchies, dictatorships, capitalist powerhouses, and being a product of the world's largest democracy, I often find myself wondering-what truly is the best model of governance?

Monarchies promise stability but often at the cost of change. Dictatorships ensure swift decision-making but silence dissent. Capitalism fuels innovation but breeds inequality. Democracies grant freedom but sometimes at the expense of efficiency. Communism seeks equality but often at the price of individual ambition. Each system, in its purest form, claims to be the best, yet none seem immune to corruption, greed, and power struggles. In the end, governance is not just about the system-it is about those who govern and those who are governed.

In democracies, much is said about the power of the people, but what use is power if wielded without wisdom? The ability to vote means little if choices are made based on emotions, caste, religion, or propaganda rather than reason, vision, and integrity. In monarchies, much is made of lineage, but what use is birthright without the burden of responsibility? In autocracies, much is celebrated about decisiveness, but what use is efficiency if it lacks accountability? And in communism, much is preached about equality, but what use is equality if it comes at the cost of freedom?

Perhaps governance is not about choosing a perfect model but about nurturing the right mindset. What if we focused less on systems and more on values? If fairness replaced favoritism, if merit triumphed over mediocrity, if leaders saw themselves as custodians rather than rulers, if people chose competence over charisma-would it really matter which system we lived under?

There is no utopia. The best governance, like the best tea, depends on the right blend-freedom with discipline, authority with accountability, progress with preservation. Nations do not fail because of their systems; they fail because of the greed, ignorance, and apathy of those who run them and those who allow themselves to be misled. Standing in the Hermitage Museum in St. Petersburg, surrounded by centuries of art, history, and power,

I realize history is nothing but a cycle of lessons we refuse to learn. From the czars to communism to capitalism, Russia has seen it all. And yet, like every nation, it continues to search for balance. Perhaps the answer to better governance is not in choosing a system, but in evolving as a people.

The Silent Conspiracy Against the Joint Family

I grew up in a house that didn't have much space but somehow held everything that mattered. A modest three-room apartment, one room for our grandparents, one for our family of four, and one for my uncle's family of four. There was no "living room" as we know it today. Whichever room was free became the sitting area. No sofas, no center tables just a rug, cushions, and all of us sitting cross-legged on the floor.

One common kitchen. One shared bathroom. One TV, an EC TV - a black-and-white box with Doordarshan as the only channel. No remote, no choices, just fixed programming. But strangely, that one channel connected all of us.

We'd huddle around the screen for Sunday evening movies, Chitrahaar, Ramayan, or the news bulletin. If someone was late, they missed it and that was that. Entertainment was communal. Meals were shared. Clothes were passed down. Arguments were real, but so was affection. Problems were discussed openly, often solved over dinner. There was no loneliness. No silent suffering. No apps. No therapies.

We didn't have a lot, but we had enough. And more importantly, we had each other.

But to the market, we were a problem

Because when families live together, they share. And when they share, they don't consume. One TV, one fridge, one mixer, one car. One family function meant everyone brought something from home, not everything bought from a store. One gift was opened and enjoyed by ten. In short, we weren't good customers.

And that's when the shift began.

Media started planting seeds. The mother-in-law became the eternal villain. Joint families were portrayed as noisy, regressive, interfering. Nuclear families were painted as modern, peaceful, aspirational. "Freedom" and "privacy" became the new mantras. The subtle message was clear: happiness lies in separation.

And slowly, we started breaking.

One joint family turned into four nuclear ones.

One home became four flats.

One fridge became four.

One kitchen became four Zomato accounts.

One black-and-white EC TV became four smart TVs with four Netflix subscriptions.

The market celebrated.

Amazon makes money when you're shopping alone on Diwali, not sitting with cousins, cracking jokes. Zomato / Talabat thrives when your mother's cooking is no longer on your plate. Netflix grows when your grandmother's stories and grandfather's advice are replaced by streaming content.

What used to be spontaneous family time became scheduled video calls. What used to be shared advice from elders became paid counselling sessions. What used to be about giving time is now about sending gifts.

Children now have their own rooms and therapists. Elders have more silence than company. Festivals have become shopping events, and love has become transactional.

We called this modernity. But was it really? Or was it just a well-packaged business model, selling us loneliness disguised as independence?

And then came another wave - the migration wave.

Children left home for better education, jobs, and business opportunities. First to bigger cities, then abroad. The family tree scattered across time zones. Grandparents became voices on the phone. Cousins became Instagram handles. Family reunions became rare, and often, awkward.

The market saw opportunity in this dispersion.

More homes to furnish. More gadgets to sell. More subscriptions to push. Loneliness became a goldmine and businesses mined it well.

If only there were enough opportunities at home.

If only good education and self-sufficiency were accessible locally. Maybe families wouldn't have had to disband in pursuit of a better life. Maybe we could've grown without growing apart.

Because when we shared lives, we shared expenses. When we adjusted with each other, we didn't spend on convenience. When we sat on the floor, we didn't need designer furniture.

And so, they sold us freedom at the cost of connection.

Looking back, I realise we weren't poor.

We were rich in values, in presence, in people.

We just didn't swipe our cards enough. And while we can't turn back time or rebuild what's been lost, we can choose differently now.

We can try to keep families close even if not under one roof. We can make time for calls that go beyond emojis and updates. We can share meals, stories, and silence whenever life allows. We can celebrate festivals with people, not packages. We can teach our children that love isn't bought, it's lived.

Maybe the biggest act of rebellion today is not buying more but sitting together, once again, in one room, around one meal, watching one screen, and just being family

The Elephant in the Room

Six blind men once met an elephant.

One felt its trunk and said it's a snake.

Another touched its leg and swore it's a tree.

One held its ear - "a fan," he declared.

Each was convinced. Each was partly right - but entirely wrong.

That's how many of us see people too. We judge by what meets the eye - a passing comment, a particular gesture, a rumour, a social media post, or just how someone dresses or speaks. We make up our minds before the full picture even shows up.

We forget that people are like elephants - not in size, but in layers. Everyone has a backstory, a reason, a struggle, a moment that shaped them. The one who seems arrogant may be shielding a wound. The one who appears distant might just be cautious. The one who's always joking might be hiding the deepest pain.

And yet, we're quick to stamp them - rude, fake, selfish, odd. One label. One moment. Sometimes, that one wrong judgment costs a friendship. Sometimes, it burns a bridge that took years to build. And worst - sometimes we never even realize what we lost.

I remember once, in a professional setting, a colleague was labelled difficult by many. He barely spoke, stayed aloof in group discussions, and always looked stern. Most people avoided him. One day, I found myself paired with him for a project. Over time, I discovered he had lost his wife recently, was raising a young child alone, and was battling insomnia. He wasn't rude - just surviving.

That changed everything for me. And it taught me a lesson I never forgot: people are fighting battles we know nothing about.

It's easy to form opinions. It's harder to pause, ask, or understand. But it's worth the effort. Because every person is more than what they seem.

Before judging - pause.

Before labelling - ask.

Before walking away - think.

We may just be touching the tail and missing the entire elephant. And life doesn't always give second chances

Reputation: The Shadow That Walks Before You

"Many a man's reputation would not know his character if they met on the street."

Unknown to yourself, you build a reputation. It takes years to earn one and seconds to lose it. A reputation is not always a true reflection of one's inner self, but once formed, it carries more weight than intentions or words. Whether earned through wisdom and sincerity or lost through arrogance and deception, it shapes how the world sees you long before you speak.

Moula Ali (AS) said, "A person is hidden under his tongue." A man's reputation is often built not just on what he does, but on what he says and how he says it. Words hold immense power-one careless statement can undo years of respect, while a single moment of honesty can etch a legacy of trust.

The Quran reminds us, "And do not let your hatred of a people prevent you from being just. Be just; that is nearer to righteousness." (Surah Al-Ma'idah 5:8). Justice and fairness in dealings protect one's reputation, while even a single act of unfairness can cast a long shadow. The world is quick to remember the times one has been unjust but slow to acknowledge a lifetime of fairness.

The Bhagavad Gita states, "A man is made by his belief. As he believes, so he is." If a person truly believes in humility, integrity, and righteousness, their actions will reflect that, and so will their reputation. But if arrogance and deceit take root, no matter how carefully one tries to mask them, they will eventually reveal themselves.

Moula Ali (AS) also said, "Your speech will tell who you are, and your conduct will define your reputation." A lifetime of virtue can be overshadowed by a single moment of weakness. People may forget a thousand acts of kindness, but they will always remember one betrayal.

History is full of examples of leaders and scholars whose reputations preceded them-some revered for their justice and wisdom, others reviled for their cruelty and deceit. A good name can open doors that wealth and power cannot. As the old saying goes, "If you take care of your character, your reputation will take care of itself." Yet, character must be guarded with vigilance, for even a small crack can break the strongest foundation.

Reputation is like glass-transparent yet fragile. Once shattered, no amount of effort can restore it to its original form. And so, whether in business, leadership, or personal life, it must be built with honesty, guarded with humility, and preserved with unwavering integrity

Right First... and Other Left-Behind Values

There's a beautiful tradition in Arab culture - "Yameen" - which literally means "right," but culturally, it stands for more than just direction. It's about deference. It's about dignity. When two people approach a doorway, an elevator, or a seating arrangement, the person on the right is offered the first move. A simple gesture, almost invisible... yet deeply graceful.

In a world that often rushes past nuance and symbolism, such customs stand as quiet reminders of what true culture looks like - not in museums or textbooks, but in everyday moments.

Having spent almost 30 years in Kuwait, I've seen how these values are not just practiced - they are lived. The way people greet one another - As-salamu Alaikum, Marhaba, Ahlan wa sahlan - it isn't mechanical. It's soulful. There's a warmth in these salutations, a sincerity that says "I see you" long before a conversation begins.

And then come the words that stay with you long after - Inshallah (If God wills), Subhanallah (Glory be to God), Mashallah (What God has willed). Not just expressions of faith, but of humility. A constant, almost poetic reminder that everything - beauty, success, even a child's smile - is ultimately beyond us and belongs to something higher.

Step into a traditional Kuwaiti household, and you'll find the culture not on display, but in action. The guest is always honoured, even if unannounced. The sitting area is always prepared, the coffee is poured, and there's always a date or a sweet to go with it - not out of show, but out of sharaf, a sense of honour.

The way elders are greeted - a kiss on the forehead, sometimes even on the shoulder - reflects a deeply rooted respect, passed down like heirlooms from one generation to the next. Not out of fear, but of affection and reverence. Not because they demand it, but because they deserve it.

The scent of oudh lingers not just in the air but in the warmth of interactions. That sitting space isn't just a room with cushions - it's a philosophy - a space for dialogue, listening, storytelling... and, more importantly, presence.

There's an old soul in every Arab home - a quiet rhythm that believes in conversation before judgment, in community before commerce. And while the modern world celebrates instant replies, breaking news, and viral trends, this part of the world still pauses to say Ahlan wa sahlan - welcome, with ease and joy.

Maybe that's what we need more of - not new ideas, but old manners. Not artificial intelligence, but real kindness. Not influencers, but elders.

Maybe, in this fragmented world, torn by noise and haste, it's time to turn right. Literally. And metaphorically.

Because "right first" isn't just about who enters a room first - it's about entering life with the right intent, the right values, and the right heart

Of Shifts, Shades, and Surprises - In Government and Boardrooms Alike

It's curious how one good experience can suddenly rewrite years of frustration.

Yesterday, someone shared a refreshing encounter at a government department in Kuwait - helpful staff, quick processing, even a smile or two. This very office, once whispered about in queues and memes, suddenly earned praise. The label shifted from "hopeless" to "impressive" overnight.

But not far behind, another person shared the exact opposite - delays, cold shoulders, missing files. The comment ended with a sigh, "What else do you expect from a government office?"

Two people. Same department. Opposite views. One jumps from 0 to 10. The other plunges from 10 to 0.

Truth is, this isn't limited to government offices. Corporates, too, ride this roller coaster every single day.

One small action - a delayed email response, an impolite receptionist, a broken promise - can trigger a spiral of mistrust. On the flip side, a single warm gesture, a solution-oriented conversation, or an unexpected follow-up can win hearts and turn skeptics into brand ambassadors.

Reputation isn't built in board meetings or budget plans. It's built in those everyday interactions - at the front desk, in the elevator, in how a complaint is handled, or how a query is closed.

People don't remember policies or press releases. They remember how you made them feel.

So, what's the takeaway?

For us - as citizens, residents, customers, clients - don't be too quick to brand or banish. One encounter doesn't define the whole. But it does offer a clue. Let's speak up when it's bad, appreciate when it's good, and share both with fairness.

For those in charge - whether of a desk at a ministry or a corner office at a multinational - remember: you're only as strong as your weakest link. Every employee is a walking-talking brand ambassador. One slip at the bottom can shake the top. One kind act can lift the whole image.

The smallest touchpoint can be the loudest message.

In the end, whether government or corporate, it's not the logo or the letterhead that earns trust - it's the people. So let every interaction count. Because somewhere, someone is writing about you today - in a post, a message, or perhaps, a little diary note like this one

The Price of Possession

A grand house, a comfortable life, yet hearts weighed down by grudges over a crumbling ancestral home. This image tells a story seen in many families-the pain of division over what was meant to unite.

Imam Ali (a.s.) once said, "Detachment is not that you should own nothing, but that nothing should own you." But how often do we forget this? In our relentless pursuit of wealth, we let it dictate our emotions, relationships, and even our love for family.

There is an old tale of a traveler who visited a wise sage. Seeing the sage's hut with only a mat, an earthen pot, a glass, a few robes, and wooden slippers, the traveler asked, "Is this all you own?" The sage replied, "And what have you brought with you?" The traveler answered, "A suitcase with three pairs of clothes and necessities." The sage smiled, "Why so little?" The traveler said, "I'm just a tourist, I don't need much." The sage responded, "So am I. So are we all. Just passing through this world."

Yet, we forget that we are mere travelers here. We hold on to grudges, fight with our own blood, and let greed cloud our hearts. Imam Ali Zain-ul-Abideen (a.s.) said, "The right of your relatives is that you maintain ties with them and not turn away from them." But how many families have been torn apart over land, money, and inheritance?

It is not wrong to build wealth or live well. But when our hearts become prisoners to possessions, when love is replaced by greed and homes by courts, it is time to pause and reflect. For in the end, no mansion, no land, no gold will accompany us-only the love we shared, the kindness we spread, and the legacy we left behind.

Let us not trade family for fleeting wealth. Let us not sacrifice love at the altar of materialism. Instead, let us strive to be wealthy in the things that truly matter-compassion, unity, and peace

The Price of Recognition-A Hollow Accolade?

In a world where achievements are measured in titles, honors, and awards, one would assume that recognition follows merit. But what happens when accolades come with a price tag?

I often receive emails and messages inviting me to accept prestigious awards-some carrying well-known names, others more obscure. They all start the same way: a flattering note about my contributions, achievements, and influence in my field. The catch? A subtle (or not-so-subtle) request for payment. It could be for "processing fees," "gala event charges," or "publication costs." But at its core, it's an invitation to purchase recognition.

How fair is that? After years of dedication, contribution, and success, must one still pay to be acknowledged? If recognition is truly deserved, should it not be honorary, given freely as a mark of appreciation rather than as a transaction?

Success in life, in any form-be it professional milestones, social impact, or personal growth-is meant to be organic. It should speak for itself. The respect and admiration of peers, the difference one makes in a community, the trust earned over decades-these are the real awards, ones that no organization can sell.

Yet, we live in times where even merit is commodified. Titles can be bought, and a self-congratulatory evening at a five-star venue can create the illusion of credibility. But does this artificial validation mean anything? True recognition is when it comes from those who matter-colleagues, society, or even a stranger whose life you've touched without realizing it.

Life teaches us that appreciation, when genuine, is spontaneous. A thank-you from a mentee, a nod of respect from a peer, a heartfelt acknowledgment from someone you've unknowingly inspired-these are the accolades that hold meaning. Not a certificate that arrives with an invoice.

So, the next time an offer to be "honoured" lands in my inbox, I'll remember real success doesn't need a paid stamp of approval. And true appreciation is never up for sale

Efficiency Before Integrity

Corruption is often called the cancer of governance. True but like any disease, it can't be cured by treating the symptom alone. The body of governance must first be made strong enough to fight it.

Imagine a simple quadrant that explains where nations and systems stand:

Bottom Left: Corruption with Inefficiency

This is where most developing systems start. Nothing moves without a push. The processes are outdated, the files pile up, and approvals crawl forward only when greased by money or influence. It's a suffocating cycle where inefficiency feeds corruption and corruption deepens inefficiency.

Top Left: Corruption with Efficiency

Oddly enough, this is the stage many systems pass through next. Work gets done quickly, but not necessarily fairly. The system is "efficient" because money oils the machine. You need something done, you pay, and it happens. It's corruption dressed up as productivity, dangerous because it feels deceptively effective.

Bottom Right: No Corruption with Inefficiency

This is the reform phase, the one that many governments step into with noble intent. Corruption is curtailed, rules are tightened, and suddenly, fear grips the system. Officials hesitate to act. Every signature feels risky. Work slows down not because people are lazy, but because they're terrified of being blamed. What was once "swift but corrupt" becomes "honest but paralysed."

Top Right: No Corruption with Efficiency

This is the ideal state - honest, transparent, and fast. Decisions are made based on merit. Systems are digitized, processes streamlined, and accountability built into every level. But you can't reach here by skipping steps. Efficiency must come first; only then can integrity sustain itself.

In today's world, time is currency. When governance delays, development stalls, and people find their own shortcuts again. The lesson is simple - to kill corruption, first fix inefficiency. Because when honest work pays as much or more than dishonest gain, the very need for corruption fades away.

True governance doesn't arise from fear of being caught. It grows from pride in doing right swiftly, fairly, and fearlessly

CHAPTER 3

RELATIONSHIPS, FAMILY & LOVE

The Many Faces of a Father – From the Eyes of a Child

It's Father's Day today. But do we really need a day to honour the quietest pillar of our lives? The unsung hero, the man who often stays in the shadows while the world celebrates others? A father's journey is unique; not just in what he does, but in how he is seen by his own child through the changing seasons of life.

I still remember watching a little boy in the park the other day, no more than four, proudly telling his friend, "My papa can lift a car!" That's how it starts, doesn't it? When we're little, our father is a superhero. He knows everything, can fix anything, and there's nothing absolutely nothing he cannot do. His shoulders are our rides to the sky, and his arms are the safest place on earth.

Then school begins, and we start learning things he doesn't know like how to use a tablet or a new game trick and somewhere the gap begins. We still look up to him, but now he's not a superhero, just someone who's always telling us to study, eat vegetables, or go to bed. We start testing his boundaries. He becomes "too strict", "too serious", or the one who "doesn't understand me". The man who once knew all answers suddenly becomes the man who "doesn't get it".

Teenage arrives with its storms. This is perhaps the most difficult phase for any father. He tries to guide, to protect, to warn; but all we hear is nagging. "He keeps repeating the same things." "Why can't he just let me be?" He becomes the embarrassing one, the outdated one, the one who's "always in a bad mood". We drift, often forgetting that he's just trying to save us from mistakes he made, paths he walked and regrets he carries. And then, adulthood happens. We face bills, job stress, heartbreaks, life decisions and slowly, almost without realising, we start echoing his words. We hear him in our warnings to our younger siblings or even our own kids. That's when we begin to understand why he said what he said. We see his wisdom. His silence that wasn't cold but cautious. His strictness that wasn't anger but protection. His irritation wasn't impatience but helplessness.

One day, when we become parents, the cycle comes full circle. We finally realise how heavy the weight of fatherhood really is. The decisions, the responsibilities, the sacrifices that go unnoticed. I recall a friend saying after his child was born, "I now understand why my father used to come home tired, still smiling, and asked about my school even when his eyes were half shut."

In old age, the man who once carried you on his back now waits for your hand to walk. His voice is softer, his pace slower, but his presence still steady. And by then, most of us finally see him for what he was all along; not a perfect man, but a man who tried, loved, worried, protected and gave, often without asking anything in return. A father is rarely expressive. He may not write you long messages or say "I love you" every day. But he'll check the car tyres before you leave, ask if you had lunch, and quietly stay up till you return home. That's his way.

To everyone reading this: if your father is around, speak to him today. Not just because it's Father's Day. Speak to him because he deserves to know that you see him. And if he's not, close your eyes, remember the lessons, the laughter, even the scoldings and smile. You carry a part of him in you.

And if you're a father yourself; know that even when it feels like your child doesn't understand you, one day they will. Maybe not today, maybe not even next year. But someday, they will see you not just as a father, but as the man who shaped their world.

That, in itself, is enough.

Once Again… Still… My Mother

Once again, today is Mother's Day.

Once again, I'll say - this day was always meant for 365.

Once again, I'll count the blessings of having a mother.

Once again, I'll show the gratitude and respect that she deserves.

Once again, I'll touch upon the countless sacrifices she made, quietly, without expecting a return.

Once again, I'll reflect on her - not just as a mother, but as the mirror of what it means to be human.

Once again, I'll go on and on… because how can I not?

Still, no words ever feel enough.

Still, I find myself short - not of love, but of language.

Still, I wonder how a lifetime of warmth, care, and selflessness can be squeezed into a few lines or a single day.

Still, she never asked for anything… and gave everything.

Still, I see her in my smallest habits - in how I care, how I forgive, how I stay quiet when it matters most.

Still, I carry her values like oxygen - unseen, but keeping me alive.

Once again, I wish her good health, peace of mind, and all the joy she never asked for but always gave.

Still, I know I can never repay her.

Still, I try - in the way I live, love, and raise my voice for what's right.

Still, I hope she sees a part of herself in me, and smiles.

So yes, once again I celebrate her.

Once again I write.

Once again I feel like words are not enough -

And once again, that feels exactly right

One Tree, Two Mothers and Endless Love.

They say nothing grows without love.

But love, too, needs to be rooted. Nurtured. Protected.

Just like a tree. Just like a mother.

Yesterday, we planted saplings at the Sheikh Sabah Al Ahmad Natural Reserve in Kuwait. It was part of a campaign - yes - but to me, it was something far more personal. It was a silent tribute to two mothers:

The one who gave me life.

And the one who keeps us all alive - Mother Earth.

Planting that sapling under the 'Ek Ped Maa Ke Naam' campaign wasn't about being part of something global. It was about coming home - to the simple truth that we owe our lives to both these mothers. One who carried us in her womb, the other who carries us all, every day.

I didn't grow up on a farm. I grew up in a joint family in the middle of Mumbai's chaos - where 10 people lived in 2 rooms, where love was loud and food was always shared. My mother didn't have time to preach about nature. But she was nature - selfless, giving, quietly enduring.

She stood like a tree - firm in storms, offering shade without being asked.

Today, we live in a world where trees are cut before they flower, and mothers are remembered more on birthdays than on ordinary days.

That one sapling I planted… was not just for the planet. It was a way of saying sorry - for all the times we take without giving back.

And a way of saying thank you - to the women who raised us, and to the earth that still holds us up.

We think we're the ones protecting the planet.

Truth is - she's still protecting us.

So plant a tree. Not for a campaign. Not for social media.

Plant it like a prayer.

Plant it like a son.

Plant it for your Ma.

Plant it for the Ma we all share - this Earth

"Plant a tree not as a gesture, but as a thank you - to the Ma who raised you, and the Ma who still holds you."

The Timeless Taste of Mom's Cooking

There's an unmistakable magic in a meal cooked by mom. For many, no delicacy in the world can quite compare to the comfort and joy found in the food prepared by a mother's hands. It's a taste that transcends the dish itself, bringing memories of childhood to life, where every bite carried the warmth of love and familiarity. Even now, long after I've grown, I still find myself reminiscing about the dishes that filled our home with delicious aromas, and if I close my eyes, I can almost taste them again.

Yet, if I were to play devil's advocate for a moment, it's worth pondering whether that magic is solely in the food or in the memories intertwined with it. As a child, I didn't know the world of flavors beyond my mom's kitchen. Her recipes shaped my palate, creating benchmarks for what tasted "good" or "bad." Dishes that delighted my young taste buds became lifelong favorites, while those that didn't appeal were dismissed, never to be revisited. It wasn't a matter of culinary skill-no Michelin-star chef could challenge the flavors that had already won over my heart. Rather, it was about familiarity, a comfort zone of tastes that became part of my identity.

This relationship with mom's cooking is, in a way, like looking back at old childhood photographs. When my boys see pictures of themselves in funny outfits from years gone by, they chuckle and wonder, "Papa, what was I wearing?" What seemed perfectly fine back then might seem amusing or out-of-date now. Times have changed, and unlike the constancy of mom's food, preferences in fashion, hobbies, and even relationships have evolved. As parents, we've learned to take a step back, allowing our children to make their own choices, from clothing to friends and even life partners. The world they navigate is different from the one we grew up in, and while some things like a mother's cooking remain timeless, other aspects of life inevitably shift with time.

Each generation has its own journey, but certain bonds remain sacred. The love woven into a home-cooked meal transcends trends, tastes, and time itself. It reminds us that while our preferences may change, some flavors, just like the memories associated with them, never fade.

What are your own experiences with this? Do you have that one dish that always takes you back home?

The Beautiful Puzzle of Sibling Differences

It's fascinating to see how two siblings, raised with the same love and values, can grow up to be so wonderfully unique. This isn't just something I've seen in others – I experience it every day with my own children too. Both are remarkable in their own ways: practical yet emotional, firm yet gentle. They share a lot, yet approach life from such distinct perspectives. It's a reminder that even in the same family, no two souls are ever quite the same.

In Islam, the soul – the ruh – is considered a gift from God, giving each individual a unique essence. The Quran says, "And they ask you about the soul. Say, 'The soul is of the affair of my Lord; and mankind have not been given of knowledge except a little'" (Surah Al-Israh 17:85). This reminds us that each soul carries a mystery, a purpose beyond our understanding. And while they may be bound by family, each soul's path is unique.

The Bhagavad Gita, too, describes the soul as eternal, distinct, and on its own journey. Krishna says, "As a person puts on new garments, giving up old ones, the soul similarly accepts new material bodies, giving up the old and useless ones." And with this journey comes accountability. In Hindu teachings, each soul is responsible for its own karma, its own actions, carrying forward the impact of those choices. The Quran similarly states, "And no bearer of burdens will bear the burden of another" (Surah Al Anaam 6:164). Each soul is ultimately responsible for its own deeds and growth.

So, if each child is unique, can we expect to raise them the same way? We may give them equal love and opportunities, but they will respond and grow in their own ways. What works well for one may feel burdensome to the other. One might thrive with structure, while the other needs freedom to explore. This requires patience, flexibility, and a willingness to see them for who they are individually.

In respecting their individuality, we honour their uniqueness and strengthen our bond with them. Siblings, in many ways, are each other's first lesson in empathy and acceptance – learning to love deeply, even with all their differences.

In the end, life is about nurturing the spark within each soul, allowing them to shine in their own way. And as a parent, there's no greater joy than watching those distinct lights grow, knowing that they each have a place and purpose in this world

From Fourteen to Two: Nest Emptied Again

An empty nest that was brimming with fourteen people just a week back, now back to two.

Lights in the house stayed on till sunrise. The kids played cards, board games, watched horror movies under blankets with popcorn bowls and half-finished coke cans lying around. They slept at 5 in the morning, just about the time I would be waking up for the day.

Mom's daily complaint remained the same - that dad forgot his before-meal medicines. Dad would sit quietly on his phone, watching reels at full volume, and when told to reduce it, he would just bring the phone closer to his ear, convinced that now no one else can hear it.

The kids danced, played, ordered food, made their own experiments in the kitchen, and enjoyed without worrying about the clock ticking away. Laundry was a minimum two-cycle affair each day. The maids had a handful to manage - clothes, dishes, bedsheets, floor - from 9 am to 9 pm without respite.

Then came the everyday question: what cuisine are we trying today? Should we order continental, Mexican, Kuwaiti, Lebanese, or Arabic street food? After all, Kuwait is known for its food - the flavours, the spices, the choices. And where would we go shopping today? Malls or local heritage markets, museums, or simply to walk by the sea.

The house was scattered with clothes, shopping bags, chargers, cables, and laptops lying on every table and bed.

Phones, smart watches, AirPods - everything had their charger spread around like small tentacles reaching for power.

And then, one day, three left. Then the next three. Then the two boys and the other four went back to their homes. The suitcases rolled out, the hugs got tighter, the eyes welled up a little, and then it was just the two of us again. Back to an empty nest.

The house suddenly seemed big and silent. No late-night laughter from the kids' room. No music blaring from the kitchen. No arguments about what to order for dinner. Just the two of us, sipping tea and thinking about those days when the house was full.

This is what joint families are about - chaos, noise, clutter, laughter, complaints, food, and an odd scolding here and there. We miss that while being away in Kuwait. We build beautiful houses here, but a house is never really a home without people filling it up with their noise and presencc.

Maybe this is what life is – swings between full nests and empty ones. Each leaving behind its own stories to smile about, sigh about, and sometimes quietly cry about too

Currency of Relationship: Love

I was listening to a lecture by a teacher of wisdom at Google. It did make sense to me, and it touched something I strongly believe in. So I thought of extending it into my own random ramblings and ruminations.

The higher purpose of life lies in the heart and soul. Are we the body, or are we in the body? Are we the mind, or are we beyond it?

Just like the crane that fixes its eyes only on the big fish and ignores the hundreds of small ones in the pond, or the hawk that dives into the lake and catches a fish in its beak; the fish was living its normal life, following its routine, perhaps swimming upstream and meeting family. It did not know it would be picked up by the hawk. Had it gone deeper within, nothing could have touched it.

So too in life, if we remain shallow, we are disturbed. But if we go deeper, we remain strong. Focus on important things that bring happiness and spread humanity and consciousness. Leave jealousy, envy, arrogance, and hatred behind.

Love is the currency of all relationships, beyond caste, creed, race, nationality, or religion. Just like all parts of the body work together to keep a person healthy, all parts of society must work in harmony. The moment one part claims it is the most important, the balance is lost, and sickness sets in. The same happens in society.

This balance extends to every profession:

For CEOs and corporate leaders, success is not only in profits but in compassion - caring for employees, customers, and communities. Once love resides in the heart, decisions naturally move from exploitation to empowerment, from short-term gain to long-term wellbeing.

For politicians, the higher pedestal is service to citizens. To govern with fairness, to treat all equally, to work for the betterment of the people. To maintain good relations with neighbours and the world at large, for peace brings progress.

For saints and spiritual teachers, the role is to guide distraught minds toward inner peace and salvation. To live with humility and modesty, setting an example first before preaching.

For doctors, healing must be with empathy, not just prescription.

For teachers, the goal is not only knowledge but shaping character.

For scientists and tech experts, the pursuit should be discovery with responsibility, remembering that the "internet" must lead us to a stronger "inner net."

Every profession, every role, has meaning only when anchored in love and service. Each of us has a role to play in this vast design. We may not all be leaders of nations or corporations, but in our daily lives; with our families, our colleagues, our neighbours; we can choose to deal in the true currency of life: love. When love fills the heart, compassion flows naturally, peace takes root, and humanity flourishes. That is the higher purpose. That is the path worth walking

Love or not Love that's the Question

The inspiration for this note came from a patio discussion over supper with a group of Gen Zs. Their perspectives were fresh, often challenging the norms I've grown accustomed to. It's fascinating how each generation reinterprets concepts like love and marriage, adding their own layers of meaning. Their insights have left me pondering, questioning, and, ultimately, appreciating the complex beauty of relationships all the more.

There's a saying that's often whispered in the context of arranged marriages: "One cares and respects their partner, but that doesn't necessarily mean they love each other." It's a thought-provoking statement, one that stirs a mix of emotions and questions. In arranged marriages, the foundation is often built on mutual respect, care, and the intention to build a life together. But does this translate into love? Or is it just a compromise?

I've always believed that love is not a single, monolithic emotion. It's layered, evolving, and often, it grows in the spaccs between care and respect. When you care for someone, when you respect their thoughts, their feelings, their essence-doesn't love quietly creep in? Or is love something grander, something that demands more than just these attributes? But where does compatibility fit into all this? We often talk about adjustments, compromise, and sacrifice as the pillars of a strong marriage, but they're closely tied to the idea of compatibility. In both love and arranged marriages, compatibility-or the lack thereof-can either ease the journey or make it a constant struggle.

Compatibility doesn't mean agreeing on everything, but it does mean that the fundamental values, outlooks on life, and personal rhythms align in a way that makes adjustments feel natural rather than forced. When there's a basic compatibility, the compromises don't feel like sacrifices; they feel like the gentle bending of two people growing closer together. Without compatibility, though, adjustments can feel like a series of exhausting negotiations, and sacrifices can build up into silent resentments. Perhaps, in arranged marriages, compatibility is something that is often hoped for, sometimes discovered, and occasionally, painstakingly forged over time. In love marriages, the initial spark of attraction might give a sense of compatibility, but as the relationship deepens, true compatibility is tested, and sometimes, it's not as strong as it initially seemed.

I've seen love marriages crumble under the weight of unmet expectations, just as I've seen arranged marriages blossom into deep, enduring partnerships. Perhaps the success of a marriage, whether arranged or love, doesn't lie in how it begins but in how the couple nurtures it. So, do care and respect translate into love? Maybe they are the seeds from which love grows. And maybe, in the context of marriage, the journey of nurturing those seeds is where the real magic happens. After all, love is not just a feeling-it's a choice, a commitment, and perhaps, a bit of a mystery that each couple unravels in their own way. As I sip on my hot chocolate at Air Canada Lounge at Montreal Airport and reflect on the stories I've seen and heard, I realize that marriage, in any form, is less about the labels we attach to it and more about the journey we embark on together. It's a dance between love, respect, care, compatibility, and yes, sometimes even compromise. But when done right, it's a dance that can last a lifetime.

A Note for My Friends: Happy Friendship Day.

To all those with whom I ran around in shorts, vests, and slippers - this one's for you.

We didn't have apps. Or gadgets. Or filters. Our filters were real, if you could race till the gate without panting, or if you were the one who could aim a stone just right to knock the mango down from the tree. Our currency wasn't digital - it was marbles, playing cards, plastic cricket balls, and sometimes even kacha aam from the compund tree. Our ambitions rarely went beyond the compound wall of the building, and yet, those felt enough.

In school, I remember sharing tiffin boxes – aloo paratha from one friend, idli-chutney from another, and that one guy who always got jam sandwiches (and never wanted to share). Notes were exchanged like secrets. Pens too. Video games with the cassettes that needed blowing into before they worked. Stamps. Cricket cards. And yes, that one incident where I helped a friend copy in physics - both of us landed with a glorious minus 10. He still owes me a samosa for that one.

Friendship wasn't a debate on religion, region, or surname. It was about who had your back when you forgot your homework, or who could climb the tree faster, or who'd guard the teacher while the rest of us played behind the cycle stand. No social background, no questions asked - just nicknames, handshakes, and unspoken trust.

College came. Fewer friends, deeper bonds. Long chai breaks. Group studies that were more group than study. The annual day chaos. That one friend who wrote everyone's assignments. The Chanakya among us who always found a way to make the impossible possible - from sneaking out at night or hostel ramblings to scoring grace marks. Some stayed, some drifted. But the real ones - they never left. We didn't need to talk every day. We just knew. The kind of friends who show up for your wedding, a family funeral, and randomly on a Sunday afternoon just because they were "in the area."

Then came work, marriage, life - the stage of acquaintances. Colleagues, clients, neighbours. A few became good friends. Some even better than childhood ones. Friendships now are not about the quantity of time but the quality of understanding. The friend who doesn't call for months but remembers your kid's birthday. The one who checks in when the news from your city or family isn't good. The one who sends a message on a random day, "Just checking on you."

Some of these were filtered over time - not by malice, just by life. But those who remain - they are gold. And to all those who read what I write here - there is a strange friendship in that too. You read, you nod, you reflect, you relate. We may not have met since long, but we've spoken - through words. That, to me, is a level of friendship that goes beyond the obvious. Like two regulars at the same coffee shop who never speak but share a nod every day. That nod is enough.

Blood relations are by birth. We don't choose them. But friends - they're handpicked over years. Through school benches and hostel beds, shared meals and shared sorrows, joys and fights. They are carved into life by conscious effort and countless small moments.

To those who walked in and stayed - thank you. To those who walked out - thank you too. You played your part. And to the ones still walking beside me - you make the journey worth it.

Here's to real friends, to those gone, those present, and those yet to come.

Happy Friendship Day

When Love Stays, Even When They Go

Life often unfolds in ways we can't fully understand. In one family, four sisters were spread across different corners of the world-two close to home and two far away. Yet, when the time came for their mother to leave this world, it was the ones living far who found themselves near, and the ones close who, for reasons beyond their control, couldn't be there. Perhaps this is destiny's way, reminding us that presence is not always about distance, but timing.

For children, losing a parent is a deeply personal and painful moment, no matter how old they are. It brings a sense of being unmoored in a world that suddenly feels much emptier. And yet, in times of grief, the bereaved don't need to be strong. They don't need to distract themselves from the loss or hold back their emotions. True healing often begins with the outpouring of tears, allowing the pain to flow freely. This release lightens the heart, providing the closure needed to begin moving forward.

I've often reflected on how the youngest in a family has a different journey with parents. The older siblings often have more time-years of knowing their parents in their strength and vitality. By the time the youngest comes of age, parents are often older, more fragile, and preoccupied with life's burdens. It can feel like the youngest gets fewer pages in the book of shared memories, and that thought can make the loss even harder to accept.

But time, as it always does, has a way of stepping in. It doesn't take away the pain, but it softens its sharp edges. Slowly, the memories that bring tears today will one day bring comfort.

This is the way life moves-a cycle of love and loss we cannot escape yet must learn to embrace.

What remains, always, is the love parents leave behind. It is in the values they instill, the lessons they teach, and the quiet strength they pass on. That love never fades-it stays, steady and unshakable, guiding us as we carry forward, even in their absence

The Bottle That Waited

This morning, while listening to the BBC World Service, one story made me stop mid-sip of my chai. A woman named Deborah, somewhere on a quiet beach in Western Australia, found an old, thick glass bottle half-buried in the sand. Inside were two notes written in 1916 by Australian soldiers heading to the First World War - Malcolm Neville and William Harley. More than a century later, their words finally surfaced.

Malcolm had written to his mother, telling her he was having a good time and that the food was fine - except for one meal they buried at sea. A young man, off to war, trying to sound cheerful so his mother wouldn't worry. He didn't come back home. He was killed in 1917, aged twenty-eight. Yet his message found its way back - carried not by the tides of the ocean, but by the quiet patience of time.

Deborah and her family managed to trace the great-grandchildren of the soldier and handed over the note. I imagined that moment - a family holding a letter from someone they had never met, yet who shared their name, their story, their blood. It must have felt like time itself took a deep breath and stood still for a while.

There's something deeply comforting about this. How things meant to happen, do happen - not always when we want, but when the universe decides the time is right. The bottle lay hidden under layers of sand, storms, and silence. It could have been lost forever, yet it wasn't. Somewhere between chance and destiny, it found its way home.

It makes me wonder about our own words, acts, and intentions - the things we put out into the world without expecting a return. A kind gesture, an honest effort, a letter never sent. Maybe they all drift around like that bottle, waiting for the right moment, the right person, the right season to reach.

So today's reflection is simple - nothing truly disappears. Not kindness, not love, not words written from the heart. They just take their own time to find where they belong. Maybe the tides of life know better than we do

CHAPTER 4

MODERN LIFE, TECHNOLOGY & CHANGE

The Wi-Fi Apocalypse: A Front-Row Seat to Social Media Chaos

If you really want to see a modern-day crisis unfold, just take away a teenager's Wi-Fi connection. Trust me, I've seen it-kids these days are glued to their phones, living their lives through Instagram, TikTok, Snapchat, and whatever new app pops up next. Losing the internet for even a second is like losing oxygen.

The other day, I was sitting in a café, sipping my latte, watching a group of teens huddled around a table. Not a single one of them was talking to each other. All eyes were on their phones, scrolling through feeds, waiting for that next dopamine hit from a like or a new follower. You could practically see them mentally calculating their social media stats. And then it happened: the café Wi-Fi went down.

I swear, you could feel the panic ripple through the room. One girl froze mid-scroll, staring at her screen like it had personally betrayed her. Another frantically tapped her phone, trying to get it to load. And then came the whisper, "The Wi-Fi's down," like it was a life-or-death situation.

They scrambled, switching to mobile data, but it wasn't fast enough for their Instagram refresh rates. Their faces showed sheer terror-what if they missed a DM? What if their latest post didn't hit enough likes? What if someone else posted a viral TikTok while they were stuck offline? You could see the *Fear of Missing Out* (FOMO) consuming them.

It's not just teens though-I've seen this drama play out with adults too. Take my friend's neighbor in Salwa, for example. One day, I saw him outside pacing with his phone, waving it in the air like he was trying to summon a signal. His Wi-Fi had cut out in the middle of a work meeting, and the desperation was real. He looked ready to declare war on the router, muttering under his breath about a "network betrayal."

Then there's my friend's son, an avid gamer. One Friday afternoon, mid-battle in his online game, the internet cut off. What followed was nothing short of an epic meltdown. "The Wi-Fi's gone!" he screamed, as if someone had pulled the plug on his entire existence. He ran around the house like he was trying to outrun the reality of his disconnected life. Watching him, I could almost feel his world crumbling around him, as if that game held the key to his future.

The truth is, these moments are everywhere. I've seen people in offices nearly lose their minds when the internet goes down during a virtual meeting. They run around rebooting routers like their lives depend on it, shouting, "Are you connected yet?!" as if their sheer willpower can bring the Wi-Fi back faster. Meanwhile, I sit back and quietly observe, sipping my coffee, amused by the chaos that unfolds every time the signal drops.

And here's the kicker-watching all these Wi-Fi meltdowns, especially with kids, you can't help but notice how deeply tied their self-worth is to these apps. It's all about the likes, the followers, the streaks on Snapchat. It's a virtual scoreboard, and they feel like they're losing if they're not constantly connected. It's no wonder they feel insecure, chasing validation from pixels on a screen, comparing their lives to the highlight reels of others.

Life Lesson:

You'd think losing Wi-Fi is just an inconvenience, but watching the reactions around me, it seems to be much more. It's like this invisible thread that connects not just devices but identities. There's a quiet kind of panic that sets in, as if the loss of connection to the internet is somehow a loss of connection to the world itself, to relevance, to purpose.

But maybe there's a lesson hidden in these moments of disconnection. When the Wi-Fi goes down, and the apps stop working, something else begins to happen. People look up. They talk to each other. They move, they fidget, and eventually, they find themselves in the real world again, awkwardly realizing that life is still happening around them, even without the screen. It's funny how we spend so much time worrying about missing out online, but in that moment, the world outside our phones is what we're actually missing.

At the same time, though, it's important to accept that the world has changed, and it's not going back. Wi-Fi, the internet, social media-they're all here to stay. The older generation may feel a sense of loss, like we've left something behind, but we also need to come to terms with the fact that this is the reality today's generation is growing up with. Internet has been a blessing for families staying across continents to stay connected and much more. Who knows, 25 years from now, the same kids we're cribbing about might be shaking their heads at the next generation, wondering why they're so obsessed with whatever new tech comes next.

It's easy to look back and say, "Things were better in our day," but that's what every generation does. Maybe what we need to remember is that just as we learned to adapt to new ways of living, today's kids will too-just on a different scale, with their own tools and tech.

In the end, the real challenge might not be disconnecting from the internet, but learning how to balance the old and the new

Of AI, News, and Noise

These days, truth is not just hard to find-it's being drowned. Drowned in hashtags, filters, clickbait headlines, and polished voices that don't always care about facts. We're living in a time where AI can make the dead speak, rewrite history, and even edit a video to make it look like someone said something they never did. A Pharaoh might rise; a Prophet might preach-but all behind a keyboard.

Social media, once a tool for connection, has slowly turned into a megaphone for noise. The louder you shout, the more views you get. The more controversial you sound, the more clicks you earn. But facts? They are often lost between opinion and outrage.

Add to that the power of AI in the hands of governments, influencers, and people with agendas. It's not just deepfakes anymore. It's smart fakes-well-crafted, believable lies that come dressed like the truth. Today, the common man is not just misled; he's overwhelmed. He doesn't know what to trust, or who.

And suddenly, everyone's an expert. Your cousin who sells shoes is now a defense strategist. The aunt who forwards recipes has become a public health advisor. The office colleague who barely passed accounts speaks like a seasoned economist. Everyone has "inside news." Everyone knows "what's really happening."

Try watching one news channel, and you feel that's the truth. Watch another, and it sounds like the complete opposite is true. Each side blaming the other. Each side accusing the other of propaganda. And somewhere in the middle, the real truth-if it exists-is quietly buried. Maybe there are bigger forces at play. Maybe none of us are really in control of the narrative.

And amidst all this, we make a mistake-we let our opinions become our barometers for relationships. "He doesn't agree with me, so he must be wrong." "She supports that side, so I'll unfollow her." We forget that people are more than their political stance or the news channel they watch. We let screens divide what conversations used to unite. That's where conformity bias slips in-they show you what you want to see, what you already agree with. And the more you see it, the more you believe everyone else is wrong.

So, here's a thought-not advice, just something I do.

I avoid channels that shout. If someone's screaming at me to believe them, they probably don't believe themselves. I stay away from forwards that begin with "Breaking News" and end with "Share this before it's deleted." I've learned to pause. Cross-check. Read the second headline. Scc who's behind the story. And most importantly, I've learned to switch off.

Silence has become rare. So has common sense.

We don't need to be experts in geopolitics or technology to know what's wrong with the world. We just need to be decent humans-curious, cautious, and aware. Ask questions. Challenge the source. Learn to dissect, not digest. That's the only way forward in a world where facts are now part of a buffet.

And if nothing works, go for a walk. Meet real people. Have a cup of tea. The world looks very different when it's not coming from a screen

The Digital Legacy

I can't help but picture a family gathered in a futuristic lawyer's office with virtual assistants and holographic presentations. The air is heavy, not with the weight of dividing immovable and movable assets, but with the inheritance of a lifetime of social media accounts.

The lawyer begins reading the will:

"I leave my Instagram account, with 8 million followers and a collection of perfectly staged sunsets and travel photos, to my eldest son. May it teach him the fine art of looking good even when life is messy.

My Facebook account, full of old family photos, birthday wishes, and forwarded jokes from 2023, goes to my youngest daughter. Use it to keep our family's memories alive, but maybe delete those old political debates.

My YouTube channel, where I documented everything from cooking disasters to successful DIY (Do It Yourself) projects, goes to my grandchildren. Turn it into whatever you like-just don't let my blooper videos go viral.

To my middle child, I leave my Twitter handle. It's a legacy of one-liners, complaints about traffic, and a few heated arguments. Use it responsibly and maybe a little more wisely than I did.

My LinkedIn profile, full of achievements and endorsements from people I barely remember, is yours to adapt and carry forward. If nothing else, it'll give you a good head start on professional networking.

Finally, my Google Photos library, filled with every important and not-so-important moment of my life, goes to all of you. It's a mess of screenshots, blurry photos, and memories, but it's yours to sort out."

By the time the will is read, the heirs might realize they've inherited not just a collection of digital assets, but a lifetime of carefully curated, and sometimes chaotic, moments. It's funny to think how things have changed. Back in my day, people passed down stories, diaries, and photo albums. Today, we leave behind followers, likes, and content streams.

But will those things matter in the long run? Will my children and grandchildren learn anything about who I truly was from my posts and videos? Or will they miss the things that didn't make it online-the real conversations, the quiet moments, the lessons I hoped they'd carry forward?

If this note survives till 2075, I hope it serves as a reminder: life isn't about perfect profiles or viral moments. It's about what you leave behind in the hearts of others.

So, dear future generations, let this be your lesson: your true legacy isn't in followers, likes, or shares. It's in the connections you build, the values you uphold, and the memories you create that no algorithm can measure.

And when you look back at my accounts, don't forget to log out and live

The Gullible OTP Saga – When a Few Digits Cost Everything

It's frightening how little it takes to lose everything.

A simple phone call, an official-sounding voice, and a carefully timed message on your phone. "Your KYC is about to expire," the caller says, "your account will be frozen." The tone is urgent, but calm-just enough to override suspicion. Moments later, an OTP arrives. You're told it's needed to "verify" your account. Without thinking, you read it out loud.

And in that moment, KD xxxxx disappears.

No alarms, no hacking drama, no suspicious link. Just misplaced trust. And that sinking feeling in the pit of your stomach when the bank confirms the transaction-you realise it wasn't a technical flaw. You handed the keys yourself.

This isn't one story. It's hundreds, happening every day. From students to seniors, from professionals to homemakers. The most common thing victims say afterward: "But I didn't share my password… only the OTP." As if that made the difference.

But the OTP is the password.

And it doesn't stop there. Some dangers don't even come with a call. They come in silence.

That free public Wi-Fi you connected to at the airport or café to save mobile data? It might've just mirrored your phone. Every photo, every contact, every app-copied without your knowledge. Your banking details, your ID scans, your location history-gone, not because you clicked anything shady, but because you trusted an open connection.

Same goes for free charging stations in malls and airports. What looks like a helpful service can be a data trap. In those few minutes your phone's plugged in, the charger could be pulling more than just battery-it could be pulling everything inside. We often guard our wallets better than our devices. But today, it's not your physical wallet they're after-it's the one on your phone.

We update antivirus software but forget to update common sense. We check if the car door is locked but blindly connect to any available Wi-Fi. We shake our heads at scam victims, thinking we'd never fall for it-until the day we do.

It's not about being naïve. It's about being human. We're wired to trust, to respond to urgency, to click before we think. And scammers know this. They don't need to be tech geniuses. They just need to sound convincing.

So here's what I've learned, painfully and through others' experiences:

- Never share OTPs. Ever.
- Never connect to unknown Wi-Fi or charge phones at public ports without protection.
- Always double-check before clicking on links or sharing information-even if it looks legit.
- If something feels rushed, stop. Verify. Call someone you trust.

Talk to your parents, your kids, your friends. Don't keep it to yourself. Shame only helps the scammers stay invisible. These days, the most secure lock isn't on your front door. It's the one on your screen. Guard it like everything depends on it-because it just might.

The WhatsApp Jungle

Being part of nearly two dozen active WhatsApp groups feels like managing a sprawling web of conversations, where everyone has a unique role. I have professional groups, advisory circles, family gatherings, friends' hangouts, management discussions, and even exclusive "men-only" and "couple-only" spaces. Not to mention the short-lived groups created for events and dinners, which disband faster than you can say "Bill settled?"

While each group has its distinct character, the personalities within them follow an amusingly predictable pattern.

THE WHATSAPP PERSONALITIES:

The Serial Forwarders:

These are the relentless couriers of WhatsApp, forwarding anything and everything that lands in their inbox. From jokes that stopped being funny a decade ago to remedies for diseases that don't exist, they never miss an opportunity to hit forward.

The Good Morning Brigade:

This enthusiastic group ensures you're greeted every morning with flowers, sunsets, and birds chirping on your screen-irrespective of the time zone. They also double up as the Happy Jumma, Happy Thursday, Happy Friday squad, with emojis that can brighten (or clutter) your day.

The WhatsApp Scholars:

Graduates from the revered WhatsApp University, these individuals know everything. From pseudo-medical advice to misquoted scientific theories, they are a walking, typing encyclopedia-albeit one with questionable accuracy. Armed with half-baked "facts" and a degree from WhatsApp University, they'll explain quantum physics, health tips, and global economics in one breath. Ask for sources, and their answer will always be: "It's everywhere; Google it!"

The First-to-Post Champions:

News doesn't break-it gets posted. Earthquakes, political scandals, celebrity updates-you hear it from them first, even before CNN or BBC. Their race to be the fastest often sacrifices accuracy, but hey, they're first! Lo and Behold! They will continue bombarding the group with news that is already aired past few hours or days on almost all channels.

The Philosophers and Motivators:

Every group has a self-proclaimed life-coach. They'll flood you with life-changing advice like Smile more or Quit complaining while grumbling about their slow Wi-Fi. self-appointed guru. They dole out life lessons, inspirational quotes, and wisdom that could rival any bestselling self-help book. They mean well, but by the fifth message of the day, you begin questioning their Zen.

The Detectives:

These are the Sherlocks, Byomkesh Bakshis, and Inspector Dayas of WhatsApp. They scrutinize every post, suspecting hidden motives or fake news. Their catchphrase: "Kuch toh gadbad hai!"

The Naïve Yet Dangerous Minds [most dangerous]:

These are the people who believe everything forwarded to them, no matter how outrageous or polarizing. Victims of propaganda and fake news, they blindly amplify divisive messages, unknowingly contributing to disharmony within groups and even society at large.

The Grammar and Fact Police:

They're the hawks of the group, lying in wait for typos, incorrect facts, or anything "off-topic." One slip-up, and they'll swoop in with corrections or sharp rebuttals. Their sharpness can turn even a harmless meme into a courtroom drama.

The Hawk-Eyed Critics:

Every group has at least one. They wait, silently, for someone to repeat a forwarded joke or send a blurry photo. Then they pounce, reminding the group: "This was already sent last week!"

The Elders of the Group:

The uncles, aunts, parents, and grandparents add their charm with blessings, anecdotes, and occasional requests for tech support ("How do you copy-paste this?"). They bring warmth, connection, and a dash of nostalgia to the chaos.

The Silent Spectators:

These are the ghost members who never comment, post, or react. They quietly observe, and their presence is only noticed when they abruptly leave the group.

The Event Planners:

Masters of coordination, these members shine in temporary groups created for dinners, trips, or parties. They juggle RSVPs, menus, and logistics effortlessly-until the group disbands, leaving no trace except a lingering question: Who hasn't paid their share yet?

The Younger Generations:

Gen Z and Gen Alpha see WhatsApp as a relic, used only to coordinate with parents or send screenshots from more happening platforms like Snapchat or Instagram. For them, WhatsApp is functional at best and embarrassing at worst. The irony? While they avoid these groups, their absence often becomes the topic of discussion: "Why don't the kids respond anymore?"

THE TAKEAWAY: A Mirror to Society

WhatsApp groups, with all their idiosyncrasies and chaos, are a reflection of life. They can foster connection, laughter, and a sense of belonging. But they also have a darker side. The unchecked spread of misinformation and propaganda in some groups creates deep divisions among friends, families, and communities. The polarization driven by fake news or politically charged forwards can erode trust and harmony, turning a simple messaging app into a battlefield of biases.

In this digital jungle, it's important to pause and reflect. Before forwarding a message or engaging in heated debates, ask yourself: Am I adding value, or fueling the fire? Technology connects us, but it also holds the power to divide. Use it wisely, for every message you send shapes the tone and impact of the group-and, by extension, the society we live in.

Let's aim to make our WhatsApp groups places of thoughtful conversation, genuine connection, and maybe the occasional harmless joke. After all, in the noise of the digital world, it's the meaningful exchanges that truly stand out

The COVID Batch: The Students Who Never Had a Normal Year

In 2020, schools around the world shut down overnight, throwing students, teachers, and parents into a new, confusing, and often frustrating world of online learning.

For the youngest ones-the first-timers in school-this was a strange introduction to education. Imagine being told that school is a magical place where you make friends, play in the sandpit, and color outside the lines… only to end up staring at a laptop screen, waving at strangers in tiny squares on Zoom. "Mute yourself" and "Can you hear me?" became their first classroom lessons.

For parents, it was a trial by fire. Homes turned into makeshift classrooms, kitchen tables into desks. Many had to juggle their own work-from-home responsibilities while ensuring their kids weren't watching YouTube instead of attending class. The battle for Wi-Fi bandwidth became an everyday struggle, and words like "breakout rooms" and "Google Classroom" became part of dinner table conversations.

And then there were the "COVID graduates"-those who spent their final years of school or university behind screens. No prom, no farewell parties, no last bench mischief, no walking across the stage in a graduation gown. Just an email saying, "Congratulations, you have graduated." Some students who had dreamt of studying abroad found themselves stuck, taking virtual courses at foreign universities while still sitting at home.

For students, the biggest rollercoaster was exams. One day, they were preparing for board exams, and the next, they were canceled. Governments and education boards kept changing decisions-first, no exams, then yes, then maybe, then back to no. Eventually, grades were assigned based on past performance, teacher assessments, and sometimes sheer luck.

COVID didn't just disrupt academics; it took a toll on mental health. Isolation, uncertainty, and the loss of a structured routine led to stress, anxiety, and even depression among students. Teachers tried their best to make online classes engaging, but the lack of human connection was undeniable.

Children who once ran around playgrounds were now glued to screens for hours, their only breaks being a quick run to the kitchen for a snack. Social skills took a hit. For two years, kids didn't have to raise their hands in class or stand up to answer a question. They could just type, "IDK" in the chatbox and move on.

When schools finally reopened, things weren't the same. Some children had never set foot in a real classroom before. They had to be taught how to share, how to sit in a classroom, and how to interact with other kids. Some even forgot how to write with a pen because they had only typed for two years.

Teachers noticed that attention spans had shrunk. Students found it difficult to sit through a full period without getting distracted. Many struggled with basics-math, writing, even social interaction. The gap in learning was real, and it would take years to fix.

For those who returned to university life, it was a mix of excitement and awkwardness. First-year students were technically in their second year but had never met their classmates in person. They recognized each other's faces from Zoom calls but felt like strangers in real life.

However, we must admit that the post-COVID education system is still grappling with a new challenge-students with shorter attention spans as mentioned earlier, an addiction to instant gratification, and a world of distractions at their fingertips. During online learning, many developed the habit of multitasking-watching YouTube while attending class, chatting with friends during lectures, and Googling answers instead of learning concepts. Now, back in physical classrooms, this digital dependence hasn't faded-it has only grown stronger.

Parents need to wake up to this reality. Social media is no longer just a pastime; it has become an alternate reality where students live, seek validation, and sometimes, lose themselves. The unrestricted access to content-whether it's gaming, influencer culture, or inappropriate material-is shaping their thinking, affecting their ability to focus, and reducing their patience for real-life interactions. Teachers can only do so much in six hours of school. The real battle begins at home.

Parents need to Set boundaries. Monitor screen time, encourage healthy discussions, and most importantly, be present. A distracted child is often an unattended one. Conversations, shared meals, and family activities need to reclaim their place in daily life. Technology isn't the enemy-ignorance is. If we don't guide them now, we risk losing an entire generation to the endless scroll of distractions.

Despite all this, the COVID generation is unique too. They adapted to a world of virtual learning, taught themselves skills outside the classroom, and learned resilience at a young age. They missed out on traditional schooling experiences, but in return, they gained something else-the ability to adapt to change.

Will this generation be different from others? Probably. They know what it's like to study in pajamas, attend classes while eating breakfast, and submit assignments seconds before the deadline-all from the comfort of their homes. They've seen how unpredictable life can be and have learned to roll with it.

As they move ahead in life, one thing is certain-they will always be known as the COVID batch. The students who graduated without sitting for exams, who entered schools without playground fights, and who learned their first lessons not from books but from a virus that changed the world.

And perhaps, in the long run, this will be their greatest strength

The Years That Tested Us.. The Years We Lost, The Lessons We Gained

It was around this time of the year in 2020 when the world was caught in a storm no one saw coming. What started as a mysterious illness in China in late 2019 soon turned into an all-consuming crisis. The words "Wuhan virus" and "coronavirus" entered our daily conversations, and before we knew it, COVID-19 had become a household name. By early 2020, life as we knew it came to a grinding halt.

Countries shut their borders. Airports looked like ghost towns. The streets, once filled with the hum of life, fell silent. Families were torn apart-some stranded in foreign lands, others locked away in their own homes. Offices, schools, and places of worship shut down. The simplest human act-shaking hands-became a dangerous gesture. Fear, uncertainty, and paranoia took over.

The search for solutions was frantic. Masks, gloves, PPE kits-things we once associated only with hospitals-became part of everyday life. In India, people scrambled for Remdesivir, believing it to be the magic bullet against the virus. In Kuwait, pharmacies ran out of Vitamin C, Zinc, and Magnesium tablets as people clung to whatever hope they could find. Some swore by home remedies-turmeric milk, steaming with eucalyptus oil, kadha, black seed oil-while others lined up for vaccines as soon as they became available. But the truth was, no one knew anything for certain.

Doctors and scientists worked day and night, trying to make sense of a virus that seemed to have its own mind. Theories flooded the internet-some scientific, others pure fiction. Conspiracy theories about lab leaks, population control, and microchips in vaccines spread like wildfire. Meanwhile, hospitals overflowed with patients, and crematoriums and graveyards ran out of space. For the first time in decades, humanity felt truly helpless.

As the world tried to regain some sense of control, a new rule emerged-PCR tests. If you wanted to travel, you needed a negative PCR result. If you tested positive, you were grounded-stuck in a foreign land, paying for hotel quarantine, waiting endlessly for another test. The PCR test industry turned into a billion-dollar racket.

Airlines, already struggling to survive, enforced strict policies. People paid exorbitant amounts for PCR tests at airports, hospitals, and private clinics-sometimes multiple times within a few days due to differing country requirements. There were stories of fraudulent negative test certificates, black-market testing labs, and travel agencies profiting off people's desperation.

And then came quarantine regulations. Some countries required 14 days of isolation-even for those testing negative. People were locked in hotel rooms, counting down the days, eating overpriced meals, and staring at four walls, wondering if they would ever return to normal life.

While millions struggled to breathe, a few saw an opportunity. Pharmaceutical giants, PPE manufacturers, vaccine producers, PCR test labs, and tech companies made billions.

Video conferencing became the new normal, and "work from home" turned into a global experiment. The stock markets, after an initial crash, bounced back stronger than ever.

But the hospitality and travel industries crumbled. Restaurants shut down. Airlines barely survived. Migrant workers in many countries lost their livelihoods overnight, forced to walk hundreds of kilometers back to their villages.

And in the middle of all this, the medical fraternity fought the hardest battle of all. Doctors, nurses, ambulance drivers, and hospital staff worked tirelessly, putting their own lives at risk. Some didn't make it. Others continued despite exhaustion, despite fear, despite the mental toll.

These were the real heroes-men and women who didn't wear capes but saved countless lives. There were also ordinary citizens who became extraordinary volunteers distributing food, people arranging oxygen cylinders, social workers ensuring medicines reached those in need. Some even gave away their savings to help strangers. If ever there was a true test of humanity, this was it.

Every evening, the world watched the COVID numbers like stock market updates. Countries were reduced to figures-cases, recoveries, deaths. But behind each number was a person-a father, a mother, a friend, a child.

The pandemic made us realize that no matter how powerful, how rich, or how advanced we thought we were, a microscopic virus could bring us to our knees. Some of the most developed nations, with the best healthcare systems, collapsed under pressure.

The virus did not discriminate. It did not care for borders, race, or status. It was the great equalizer.

And yet, as with every storm, this too passed. Vaccines rolled out, and bit by bit, life limped back to normal. Masks were removed. Lockdowns lifted. People returned to their offices, and children to their schools.

But we were not the same. Some had lost loved ones. Others had lost livelihoods. Mental health had taken a hit. The scars, both seen and unseen, remained.

Looking back now, the pandemic feels like a chapter from history-just like the Spanish Flu a hundred years ago. The world moved on, as it always does.

But if there's one thing COVID-19 taught us, it's that life is unpredictable. Plans mean nothing when the unexpected strikes. And in the end, it's not wealth, power, or status that truly matter. It's health. It's human connections. It's kindness. And live your day. Don't wait for tomorrow. Enjoy today.

May we never see such a catastrophe again. But if fate wills otherwise, may it not be for another hundred years. And when that time comes, may we be better prepared-not just with science and medicine, but with compassion, wisdom, and a deeper understanding of what truly matters.

And to the good Samaritans-the doctors, nurses, volunteers, and strangers who became saviours-may God bless them abundantly. The world owes them a debt it can never truly repay

The Gym, the Walk, and WhatsApp University

Health and fitness gurus keep telling us - give yourself at least 45–60 minutes daily. Walk, meditate, do yoga, swim, hit the gym, or at least stretch a bit, they say. Alongside, eat right, sleep well, and uplift your soul with prayer or reflection. Simple, isn't it?

Well, not really. Yesterday with close friends, I was boasting about my "disciplined" routine - waking up at odd hours, finding inspiration to pen down my RRRs, and then heading to the gym. But before my friends could admire me, I quickly clarified: the results don't quite show! Maybe because I skip the gym on alternate days (my excuse: rest and recovery) or because evenings are a nightmare; full of buffed-up guys who make me feel like a timid visitor in a gladiator's arena. So, I switched to mornings. Except there, the walking track is ruled by cheerful 70-year-olds in animated discussions about politics and pensions. Hard to get inspired for a 45-minute sweat session when you're surrounded by laughter and gossip.

Tried going with best friends - but that ended up as more socialising than exercising. Tried walking - but then Instagram reels and WhatsApp University enlightened me: walking doesn't build muscle, nor does it extend life. After all, crocodiles, hippos, elephants, rhinos, pandas, and bears all live long lives without walking marathons!

So, the new prescription? Stay in bed as much as possible. Go to work, sit behind the desk, return home to the couch, then surrender again to the bed. With a brief stopover at the dining chair and the "commode chair." Add a detox of ginger-lemon-parsley-coriander water, and voilà - no need for doctors! Thank you, WhatsApp University. You've saved us all.

This is the same university that teaches us politics, spreads "social truths," reinforces conformity bias, and provides "educative information." Health is just the latest subject added to its syllabus. And like obedient students, the naive and the educated alike enrol - tuition-free.

It reminds me of the old slogan "Padhega Bharat, toh Badhega Bharat" (If India studies, India will progress). But with this new-age WhatsApp syllabus, maybe we should update it to "Forward karega Bharat, toh Badhega Bharat" (If India forwards, India will progress).

Until then, I'll keep juggling between the gym, the walk, the sofa, and the bed and let WhatsApp be my professor

The Art of Shopping: Between Needs, Wants, and a Debt Trap

It's one thing to shop wisely, another to shop recklessly, and a whole different game to shop on borrowed money.

A gentleman I know has come to me multiple times, asking for a loan. Every time, the promise is the same: "Just six months, and I'll return it." This time, I finally asked, "What's the urgency?"

Turns out, he needed to repay someone else from whom he had borrowed earlier. And why did he borrow in the first place? To buy a new phone. Not just that-he had installment payments pending for gadgets from an electronics store. He had stretched himself so thin that he now risked being blacklisted.

This is how debt creeps in-not for survival, but for indulgence. You buy things you don't need, with money you don't have, only to realize later that you're stuck in a cycle. Borrowing to repay borrowing, struggling to make ends meet.

It reminds me of a fourth-grade lesson from 1978. A mother-in-law visits her daughter's house and is impressed by the refrigerator, television, and all the fancy new gadgets. "How do you afford all this?" she asks.

The daughter replies with a smile, "Everything is on installments."

The old lady does some quick math and says, "You're paying so much in EMIs that it equals your entire income. What about your basic needs?"

Fast forward to today, and the situation has only worsened. The world is full of glitter and glamour, and the pressure to keep up with others is immense. Social media makes it even worse-if your friend gets a new car, you want one. If your colleague upgrades his phone, yours suddenly feels outdated. But the real question is, do you actually need it? Can you afford it without sinking into debt?

I once saw a man holding his wife's hand all through a mall. It looked like love and affection-until a friend congratulated him. He sighed and whispered, "It's not love, my friend. Every time I let go of her hand, she buys something, and my card gets swiped."

That's modern shopping in a nutshell. But it doesn't have to be this way.

Our scriptures emphasize contentment. They don't say one should live miserably, but they do stress living within one's means. Buy good things, but only if you can afford them. Wear the best, but not at the cost of your peace. Avoid unnecessary loans, EMIs, and especially interest-based debts that can silently destroy financial stability.

The Bhagavad Gita reminds us:

"A person who is not disturbed by the incessant flow of desires-that enter like rivers into the ocean, which is ever being filled but is always still-can alone achieve peace, and not the person who strives to satisfy such desires." (BG 2.70)

The Manusmriti states:

"One should enjoy wealth with detachment, for wealth, like a passing cloud, is never permanent."

– (MS 4.16)

Islamic teachings also emphasize avoiding interest-based transactions:

"Allah has permitted trade and has forbidden usury (interest)."

– (Quran 2:275)

Moula Ali (AS), known for his wisdom, beautifully described the balance between wealth and life:

"Do not be a slave to others when Allah has made you free."

– (Nahjul Balagha, Saying 426)

He also said:

"Do not be like the person who hopes for the Hereafter without action, and delays repentance through long hopes. He speaks like the ascetic in the world but acts like those who desire it. If he is given something, he is not satisfied; and if he is deprived, he is not content." (Nahjul Balagha, Sermon 150)

His great-grandson, Imam Zainul Abideen (AS), highlighted the balance between spending and frugality:

"The best of wealth is that which saves your face and satisfies your needs." (Risalat al-Huquq – The Treatise on Rights)

The true art of shopping isn't just about finding the best deals-it's about knowing when to buy, what to buy, and when to walk away. Because at the end of the day, no one else will earn for you, no one else will pay your debts. It's you and only you. And the world? It will clap when you show off, but it won't come to help when you struggle

Dollar Value

Something's been bothering me of late. Maybe it's age, maybe experience, or maybe just fatigue from pretending not to notice the obvious. Three decades in the profession and the faces have changed, but the game hasn't.

Over the years, I've sat across the table from industry veterans, visionaries, IIT/IIM prodigies, and "LinkedIn lions" with award-winning bios. They talk of strategy, ethics, innovation, leadership… all the usual buzzwords. But strip the jargon and a pattern starts to show.

People look at you like a price tag. A walking talking profile snapshot. Are you worth their time? Their greeting? Their invite to that exclusive event? Do you sit in a boardroom or in the audience? Do you know someone worth knowing? Have you been photographed with ministers m, business tycoons or CEOs? Because if you have, you must be important.

If your profile has titles, if your followers cross a few thousand, if you're called to speak at forums or flagged by a media article, you're treated with a different tone. One of respect - not necessarily for who you are, but for what you are in that moment. But does that define you?

If tomorrow, all those badges are taken off, would they still call? Would they care? Would they even remember your name without scrolling?

Sometimes I look at my LinkedIn list. Thousands of connections. But how many would actually know me beyond the summary line? How many have shared a real conversation, a worry, a meal, a laugh?

There's a strange sort of loneliness that success brings. The more decorated your profile, the more transactional your relationships become. People approach you with a purpose. They meet to network, not to connect. They message not to say "how are you," but "can you help me with…"

And corporates, they talk about values and social responsibility with so much chest-thumping, yet fire people for a private hug caught on camera, or for cracking a joke out of line with company image. Are we hiring humans or robots? Does morality now come with a disclaimer?

Real relationships - they're found elsewhere. In old classroom benches. In hostel corridors. In canteens where we had to share a samosa because someone was broke. When dreams were unpaid and friendships were unconditional.

Back then, no one asked your designation. No one filtered you based on pay scale. Everyone knew each other's story, not summary.

Today, I find myself longing for that simplicity. For someone to pick up the phone not because I'm the CFO or Chairman or Fellow of something, but just because they thought of me. No agenda. Just a hello.

Maybe that's the irony of the professional world - we work all our lives trying to climb ladders, only to find the view is crowded, cold, and mostly fake.

And somewhere in all that climb, we forget what we were climbing for in the first place

Embracing Consumer Surplus and a Cheat Budget

Today, I found myself reflecting on the concept of consumer surplus and how it can weave its way into everyday moments. It struck me that life is not just about strict regulations and rigid budgets; it's also about easing up, indulging in the little things, and understanding the value of flexibility.

I've always had a sweet tooth. Whether it's a sprinkle of sugar in my tea, a piece of chocolate in the evening, or a scoop of ice cream on a hot day, these small pleasures bring joy. Instead of seeing them as guilty pleasures or "breaking" my 2000-calorie limit, what if I framed them as part of my cheat budget? By allowing myself these treats, I give myself some extra space. It's not about the calories; it's about the happiness they bring. Life is too short to deny myself the joys I love.

This mindset can extend beyond food. Think about the little everyday encounters, like taking a taxi. If the agreed fare is KD 2, and the driver asks for KD 2.5, what's the harm? Sure, it's a little more than expected, but maybe he's relying on that extra half dinar to get by. Instead of letting frustration bubble over, I could simply shrug it off. For just 500 fils, why let it ruin my day? Keeping a little extra cash for these moments allows me to embrace them without guilt.

Consumer surplus is simple yet profound. When I plan to spend a certain amount but find something cheaper, the difference is a small victory, a moment of grace. It's the thrill of getting a good deal, but it's also about the mindset. If I walk into a shop ready to spend KD 5 on a treat only to discover it's KD 3,

I've gained that surplus. I feel good because my expectations were met with a pleasant surprise.

So, here's to creating my own cheat budget, to savoring those little indulgences without the burden of guilt. Here's to finding joy in being generous with myself-whether that's through sweet treats or extra fare for a taxi driver. Instead of allowing anger or resentment to seep in when things don't go as planned, I'll focus on the positives and keep my heart open.

Today, I choose to embrace consumer surplus in all its forms. I choose to enjoy life's little pleasures without holding back. And in doing so, I remind myself that happiness often lies in the spaces between rules, in the joyful acceptance of life's little surprises.

Until next time

Awe of Today's Pronoun Revolution, Gender Identity, and Changing Perspectives

I recently noticed a professional acquaintance-using 'she/her' in his email signature. It got me thinking about how gender identity has evolved, and I'm in awe of how freely people today choose to define themselves. It's not uncommon now to see a man identifying as 'she/her,' a woman using 'it/their,' or individuals opting for gender-neutral terms. What once seemed unshakably binary has now expanded into a broad spectrum of identities.

Traditionally, gender was binary: male and female. Ancient scriptures reflected this understanding, whether in Hinduism's Purusha (male) and Stri (female), the Bible's "male and female He created them" (Genesis 1:27), or the Quran's recognition of both men and women, (Surah Al-Hujraat 49:13). There was also acknowledgment of a third gender in some texts, like the Tritiya-prakriti in Hinduism, representing those outside the binary-eunuchs or hermaphrodites, for instance.

However, today's world recognizes that gender is not solely defined by biological sex. Gender now is defined grammatically or naturally. The concepts of gender-neutral and non-binary have become part of the conversation. Gender-neutral refers to terms and identities that avoid specifying male or female traits, such as using 'they/them' pronouns. Non-binary goes beyond this by rejecting the strict male-female divide altogether, encompassing various identities like genderqueer, genderfluid, or agender, where one's sense of gender may be a mix of male and female or even outside these categories entirely.

To many, this represents progress-an inclusive approach that allows individuals to define themselves on their own terms. The freedom to choose one's pronouns and identity gives a voice to those who felt constrained by the traditional male-female framework. Yet, as I see individuals-some with traditional roots-adopt these identities, I wonder if this newfound liberty is challenging us to reconsider age-old perceptions, or if it risks unravelling the clear boundaries that once provided structure.

Freedom today means more than it ever did; it's not just about choosing how to live but about how to be. Whether this shift ultimately adds to the richness of human experience or dilutes the meaning of identity itself remains an open question.

I'm no judge here, but as I see more people-some from traditional backgrounds-embracing this change, I can't help but reflect on whether this newfound liberty is reshaping or simply unravelling the structures we once held sacred. It's a profound shift, and I'm left in awe of where it will take us next

Fraud: The Art of Deception, Then and Now

As a child, I learned a hard lesson about trust. Sent to buy a tin of Lactogen for my baby brother, I was stopped by a man who pointed out a dent in the tin. He offered to help me exchange it, walked with me to the medical shop, and suggested I take a different route while he carried the tin. I waited at the store, but he never showed up. That was the day I lost more than just a tin of Lactogen-I lost a bit of my innocence.

Fraud has always been about deception, playing on trust and exploiting gaps in awareness. What started with small cons on the streets evolved into email scams about lottery winnings and wealthy widows needing help to transfer millions. Then came fake job offers, phishing messages, OTP frauds, and now, deepfakes-where AI can mimic voices and faces so convincingly that even seasoned professionals have fallen for it. A London-based company recently lost millions because its staff received a video call from what appeared to be their CFO. It wasn't him. It was AI.

For a generation that grew up in a world of face-to-face interactions and handwritten letters, the digital age feels overwhelming. Many still hesitate to trust online banking, digital payments, or automated systems. But the truth is, avoiding technology is not the solution. The fraudster no longer waits at a pan shop or a busy street corner. He now sits behind a screen, masked by an email, a video call, or an AI-generated voice.

Takeaways for Those Still Acquainting Themselves with Tech:

1. Scams are not new, only their methods have changed.
2. Technology is a tool, not a threat-but like fire, it must be handled with care.
3. Trust is good, but verification is better.
4. If something feels too good (or too urgent) to be true, pause and think.

The world has changed and so have fraudsters. The only way forward is to stay aware, ask questions, and embrace technology with caution, not fear. The elephant is in the room-we must learn to live with it safely

CHAPTER 5

HUMOUR, IRONY & EVERYDAY OBSERVATIONS

The Other Side of Presence

Outside a church in Mumbai, I came across a line: "Life without love is like pav without vada."

For those unfamiliar, pav is the soft Indian bread roll, and vada is a spiced potato fritter. Together they form vada pav, a simple yet iconic street food of Maharashtra. Remove the vada, and the pav is just plain bread. Take away the pav, and the vada stands incomplete. Their absence reveals their need, their presence makes them whole.

Life is no different. Darkness is nothing but the absence of light, and it is this very absence that teaches us the value of its presence. Silence, in its absence of sound, reminds us of the presence of words and voices. Illness, through the absence of health, magnifies the presence of well-being. Loneliness, the absence of companionship, sharpens our sense of the presence of togetherness.

Absence is not just emptiness - it is the mirror that shows us what presence truly means. And presence, in turn, carries weight only because absence exists.

That playful line outside the church was not only about bread and fritters. It was a gentle nudge, reminding us to notice both: what is present and what is absent and how, together, they give life its meaning

The Tougher Test of Success

They say failure is hard to handle. I disagree. The only thing harder to handle than failure is success.

Failure humbles you, teaches you, and even earns you sympathy. People gather around to console you with kind words, "Don't worry, better days will come." But success? That's a different story. Success attracts applause in public and whispers in private.

I've seen people rise quickly in different walks of life - fame, recognition, position, or status. At first, they were grounded and approachable. But once success arrived, something shifted. Their greetings became longer, their laughter became louder, and even small achievements were narrated like historic milestones. Success does that - it slips a crown on your head and waits to see if you'll carry it lightly or let it press down with weight.

Success is a double-edged sword. One side cuts you with ego and pride; the other side cuts you with envy and jealousy from others. It is like walking across a rope bridge: lean too much one way and you fall into arrogance, lean the other way and you fall into isolation.

Failure, at least, allows you to retreat quietly. Success drags you into the spotlight. And the spotlight is hot - it magnifies both your strengths and your stumbles. One mistake after success feels ten times louder than ten mistakes during failure.

A few truths I've picked up along the way: Failure introduces you to reality; success introduces you to critics you never knew existed. Failure teaches you patience; success tests your tolerance. May be God's way of testing you.

The secret is simple: stay grounded, stay humble, and thank the Almighty at every step. Laugh at yourself before others do it for you. Carry success like salt in food - just enough to add taste, never so much that it spoils the dish.

We are taught again and again how to cope with failure. But maybe we should stop asking, "How do you cope with failure?" The tougher and more important question is, "Can you handle success?"

On Perception

Mathematics, science, astronomy - all so precise. Two plus two cannot suddenly become five, no matter how many PowerPoint presentations one makes. If the Earth decided to wobble off its axis by even a micro-nano-second, we'd all be colliding like bumper cars at a funfair. That's the comfort of science: precision, predictability, and one right answer.

But step into the world of art, aesthetics, and daily life - suddenly, there is no "right" answer. Perception takes over. Someone loves black, someone blue, someone insists that red is the colour of passion. Does that make the others wrong? Of course not. Some like tea, some coffee, and some prefer neither but still show up at the coffee shop just to gossip. Some crave mountains, others the sea, though frankly, in Kuwait we've only got the sea, so perception here is limited by geography.

Perception is that strange lens through which we all see life differently. As children, we thought money was everything. As teenagers, we thought freedom was everything. As adults, we realize sleep is everything. Perception changes with time. What once looked like a "career-defining opportunity" may later look like "a masterclass in stress management." And that boss who once seemed terrifying might later be remembered as just another over-caffeinated human juggling deadlines and domestic drama.

Even at IBPC, I've seen how perception plays out in the funniest ways. One member looks at an event and says, "What a fantastic networking opportunity." Another says, "Too many speeches, not enough food." And a third says, "Why was I seated at the back table?" Same event, same evening, three entirely different perceptions. And yet, all are valid. You can't really argue with hunger, boredom, or ego - they all have their own truth.

Take politics too. A politician makes the same speech to three audiences: one calls him a visionary, another calls him a liar, and the third is just worried about when lunch will be served. The words didn't change - perception did. Or take the office email. One person reads it as polite, another as rude, and the third doesn't read it at all but hits "reply all" with "Noted."

Life is full of such perception-driven comedy. A parent thinks their child is glued to the phone for nonsense, while the child insists, they are "networking" or "researching." The neighbour who parks his car half a foot into your space thinks it's no big deal, while you think it's grounds for World War III. The same street food - golgappa at Sargam or shawarma from Kurdos, that you loved at 30 now makes you reach for antacids at 50. Perception shifts with age, metabolism, and cholesterol levels.

The real danger comes when we mistake our perception for the universal truth. My tea-loving conviction doesn't make the coffee drinker inferior. My love for classical music doesn't give me the right to sneer at someone's playlist of remixed Bollywood songs. Debate, discussion, even disagreement is healthy. But abuse, berating, or worse - violence - over differences in perception is the real tragedy of our times.

So, maybe the lesson is this: respect that perception differs. Argue if you must, laugh about it if you can, but never impose. Because the same rainbow we all admire has seven colours, not one. And no one ever stood beneath a rainbow complaining, "Why is it not just my favourite colour?"

In the end, life is less about proving who is right and more about understanding where the other is coming from. Perception may change, but humanity must remain constant. And if nothing else, remember - your spouse's perception of how much salt you put in the food will always be different from yours. Accept it, smile, and pass the pickle

Ramblings under the Blood Moon

Yesterday, the skies put on a show – a total lunar eclipse, often called the blood moon (6.25 pm to 11.55 pm Kuwait Time). The word eclipse itself comes from the Greek ekleipsis, meaning "abandonment" or "failure to appear." In a way, it's almost poetic - the moon doesn't really disappear, it only borrows the earth's shadow for a while, reminding us that even absence has its place in life.

Traditions around the world have always given the eclipse a certain weight. In India, elders would often ask us to stay indoors, avoid food during the eclipse, or chant prayers. In other parts of the world, people saw it as an omen, a warning, or a shift in power. I remember, as children in school, we'd secretly slip out onto the terrace with pieces of x-ray film or a bowl of water to "safely" watch the moon's color change. The excitement wasn't just about science, it was about watching something bigger than us unfold in the heavens.

Scientifically, of course, it's simple. The earth comes between the sun and the moon, casting its shadow. The red tint is just sunlight filtering through the atmosphere, scattering blues and leaving behind shades of copper and crimson. But somewhere between the textbook explanation and the hushed whispers of tradition lies the beauty of it all.

Life too has its eclipses. Times when our own light is dimmed, not because we have lost it, but because circumstances have cast a shadow over us. Like the moon, we don't stop existing. We wait it out, and when the shadow passes, we shine again.

I've seen this in ordinary moments. A friend once struggled through CA exams, convinced he was "finished," only to come out stronger once the shadow of doubt passed. At work, too, there are phases when no matter how hard you try, recognition doesn't come. But just like the moon, patience helps – the shadow moves on eventually.

The eclipse also teaches humility. The mighty moon, worshipped, written about in poetry and songs, spends a few hours hidden, reminding us that no one shines all the time. And maybe that's how it should be. Just as nights without electricity in our childhood made the stars brighter, our own pauses and struggles make our brighter days more meaningful.

So tonight, as the moon turns red, I think of it less as a celestial event and more as a mirror of life. Shadows will come, sometimes longer, sometimes shorter, but never permanent. And when the shadow lifts, we'll remember that even during the darkest eclipse, the moon never stopped being the moon

Coincidence, Accident, or Destiny?

Meeting people is one of the simplest yet most mysterious parts of life. We cross paths with so many - at social gatherings, conferences, family functions, even while waiting outside classrooms during a parent-teacher meeting. Some we exchange business cards with, some we exchange pleasantries with, and with some, the interaction ends as quickly as it begins. But with a few, something clicks. We connect, we gel, we feel at ease. The conversation flows as if it was waiting to happen.

Now the question arises - are these meetings mere coincidence, an accident of timing, or something destined? Perhaps it's a mix of all three. Coincidence puts us in the same place, accident allows a moment of interaction, and destiny chooses which of these moments will grow roots. That's how societies, communities, and friendships are formed - through connections that survive beyond the initial meeting. Do we choose our connections, or do they choose us? Maybe both, maybe neither. Maybe they simply happen.

Interestingly, it's not always with like-minded people. Many times, we gel with those who are completely different from us - different temperaments, different interests, even different values at times. Yet, the bond grows. That is the strange beauty of human connections; they do not follow logic, they follow a rhythm of their own.

Looking back, each one of us can recall such meetings that changed the course of our lives; friendships that became families, acquaintances that became lifelong allies. The rest simply remained faces we once met. And that too has its own place.

This note today is for all those who stayed on in our lives, who became our closest circle, our trusted companions, our besties who know us as we are. Think of them today. Tell them how much you value them, how grateful you are to have them, and how fortunate it feels that what could have been just another passing encounter, became a lasting bond.

Because whether it was coincidence, accident, or destiny - it was meant to be

An Obituary for English Literature (With a Lewk at the Future)

Today I write an unusual obituary - not for people, but for the torchbearers of English literature. With delulu, skibidi, tradwife, and lewk making their way into the Cambridge Dictionary, I can almost hear a collective groan from the greats. If they had tombstones that spoke, they might read something like this:

Here lies William Shakespeare, slain not by daggers or poison, but by "skibidi."

Here rests Charles Dickens - who gave us "It was the best of times, it was the worst of times"… and now would surely add, "it was the most delulu of times."

Here sleeps Jane Austen, who wrote of sense and sensibility, but never of lewks and aesthetics.

Here lies John Keats, who sought beauty in truth - only to see beauty replaced by emojis

And yet, this is not really a tragedy. It is simply the story of language doing what it has always done - evolving, adapting, reflecting the times.

Fast-forward to 2050, and perhaps our grandchildren will laugh at us for treating these Gen Z and Gen Alpha words with such fascination. Just as today's youngsters marvel at black rotary phones, bulky radios, or thick Oxford dictionaries, tomorrow's kids will see our obsession with slang as quaint, maybe even charming.

Is this good or bad? Only time will tell. But one truth stands firm: change is the only constant. Every generation writes its chapter - in art, literature, society, and technology. The words may differ, but the contribution remains.

As for us, we may learn a few of these new expressions, if only to stay in touch with the times. But our philosophy and outlook will remain shaped by the generation we belong to. That's not a flaw - it's the rhythm of history.

So instead of mourning the past or mocking the present, perhaps it's better to smile, embrace the absurdities, and tip our hats to change. Because in the end, whether the word is lewk or loquacious, language is just the vessel; the real treasure is the story it carries

Godman Inc. – Heaven for Sale, No Complaints Registered

I felt like penning this down today when I came across a post - a firangi baba (a foreign spiritual guru, usually seen as someone imitating or capitalizing on Indian traditions) blessing a newly married Indian couple. Robes on, hand raised in blessing, and a serene expression that looked straight out of a movie set. A friend had rightly commented, "When the business is this profitable, even foreigners are launching startups." That line stuck. And made me think deeper.

Not out of mockery, but out of concern. Not for the godman, but for the people.

Godmen or let's say spiritual gurus often start out as ordinary folks. Somewhere along the way, they claim to have found enlightenment. And with that, begins their journey, from a seeker to a speaker, and eventually to someone who's followed without question.

Now, let me be clear. This isn't about all of them. Some may be genuine. But many are not.

And it's the conmen in robes I'm writing about the ones who've mastered the art of selling faith, wrapped in mysticism, garnished with fear, and served with a side of confidence.

No boundaries of religion, language, or region here. These thugs come in all colours - saffron, white, green, black - whatever the audience demands. Their sermons are carefully worded, their solutions quick-fix, their charm convincing. And their ultimate aim? Not your soul. Your surrender.

They thrive where logic fails. They know people will come, especially when they're lost, scared, or desperate. And when you're in that place, reason takes a back seat. You follow. You donate. You obey.

From there begins the empire - disciples, wealth, centres, events, blessings-for-a-fee. Then come schools, hospitals, environmental projects - not just for service, but for optics. Politicians join in. Cameras flash. Governments sometimes fund. All this while, the public image is that of a healer, a giver, a divine figure.

And if something dark comes up - a scam, a crime - it's covered up. Followers defend. Courts delay. The godman meditates behind bars. Returns as a hero.

It's a full-proof model. The only product being sold is heaven. And guess what? No one ever comes back to complain that it wasn't delivered.

That's why I wrote this today. Not to offend anyone. But to remind everyone - to pause and think. Ask questions. Don't hand over your life to someone just because they speak slowly, smile often, and dress differently.

*True faith doesn't need a middleman.

True spirituality doesn't ask for your wallet.

And real gurus don't ask you to stop thinking.*

Beware of those who speak of god but act like businessmen. Not all who preach are pure. And not every robe hides a saint

Sixth Freedom Passengers...

At home today, I was explaining to mom how flights work - how a direct flight from destination A to B is straightforward, but how some flights go via another country, pick up passengers, and continue onwards. Someone casually remarked, "You know what that's called? Sixth freedom passengers."

And as usual, this simple term made me pause and ponder.

Sixth freedom passengers...

But People who start somewhere, transit somewhere else, and reach somewhere entirely different.

Isn't life like that too?

We think we are headed straight from our dreams to our destinations. But life often takes us via unexpected stops - a job we didn't plan, a city we never thought we'd live in, a person we didn't expect to meet or a failure that became the runway to our next success.

In business too, how often do we design a direct route, but end up taking via routes to reach our goals. Sometimes, these via routes are not diversions, they are essential transits that connect us to opportunities we could never have imagined.

In life too, be open to becoming someone's via point. You may not be their destination, but your role in their journey could change their world.

As a teacher, mentor, friend, leader, colleague, or even as a stranger with a smile at the right time.

Sixth freedom passengers reminded me that freedom itself lies in embracing these indirect paths, these unplanned transits, these short halts that give us fuel, perspective, and new wings to fly further than we ever imagined.

Just some random ramblings and ruminations…

Because the shortest distance between two points is a straight line, but the richest journeys rarely are

Sitaarein Zamein Par

Last evening, as part of IBPC's summer calendar, we hosted a screening of Sitaare Zameen Par for our members and their families. In this Kuwaiti heat, it was more than just an escape-it was a gathering that warmed the heart. Familiar faces, informal chatter, popcorns and Drinks and that hush when the lights dimmed and the screen lit up.

The movie? It held you without shouting. No over-the-top drama. Just moments. Lines. Silences.

And those one-liners… some of them stayed long after the end credits.

"Sabka normal alag hota hai."

Everyone's normal is different.

We throw around words like "abnormal", "different", or worse - without thinking. But what's routine for one may be a mountain for another. And vice versa. That one line hits like a quiet truth. No judgement. Just perspective.

"Ghar budha ho jaata hai jab bacche chhod kar chale jaate hain."

A house begins to age the day its children leave.

Not dramatic. Just matter-of-fact. The house doesn't complain. But the clock ticks louder, the fridge feels too full, and every closed door echoes differently. We don't notice the ageing, until it quietly settles in corners.

"Hum doosri team ki beizzati karne nahi aaye… hum jeetne aaye hain."

We didn't come to insult the other team… we came here to win.

Rare to hear this in any field now. More time is spent pulling the other down than playing your own game. This line was refreshing. Play to win, not to destroy. Compete, not compare.

"Main team kaise banu… team toh normalon ki banti hai na?"

How can I build a team? Teams are made by "normal" people, aren't they?

Said with sarcasm, but it cuts deep. Who decides who fits and who doesn't? So often we disqualify ourselves before trying - because someone somewhere made us feel like we didn't belong.

"Coach acche ho… lekin aadmi suar ho."

You're a good coach… but a terrible human being.

No politeness. No filters. And rightly so. Skills don't mean much when you've forgotten basic decency. The line made the whole hall go silent. Sometimes the truth needs no polish.

"Paagal ko paagal bhi na bolein? Ye kya baat hui?"

We can't even call a madman mad? What nonsense is this?

The kind of line that people use to hide behind insensitivity. And yet, it makes you think - why do we feel the need to label every difference? Is it really so hard to just be kind?

And then the moment that made everyone in the theatre smile:

"Hum jeete hain… doosre number pe."

We won… at second place.

Simple. Honest. Dignified. They didn't accept defeat - not because of denial, but because they recognised the win in their journey. That attitude, that pride-it stayed with me.

The movie ended. The lights came on. People clapped, some stretched, others lingered in their seats. All thanked and praised us for organising the screening.

But something stayed behind. A few words. A few truths. A few reminders. That maybe, just maybe, life isn't about medals or labels. It's about showing up. With courage. With grace. And with the quiet confidence that your story, too, matters.

Sometimes it takes a simple film on a warm evening to remind us - It's okay to come second. It's okay to feel. It's okay to not fit someone else's idea of 'normal.'

And maybe, just maybe, that's how we keep the stars shining. Even if not all of them are in the sky

From a Convocation Day

Some days stay with you; not because they're loud, but because they stir something quietly inside. Today was one of those as I sat at the UOttawa Faculty of Engineering convocation, watching my boys graduate. Five / Six years of effort, growth, and life rolled into one neat ceremony with black gowns and proud smiles.

The President and Vice Chancellor gave a speech that stuck with me more than I expected. He said something like:

"Five years ago, you didn't know where the library was. Where the labs were. You didn't know your professors, or your classmates. You came here knowing no one. And today, you leave with friends who will stay with you for life."

That hit a nerve. Maybe because I saw it in my sons' faces. Or maybe because I was pulled back to my own life, my own memories of leaving college, stepping into the "real world" where things aren't laid out in a syllabus.

These five years, full of firsts and full of 'news'. New country. New friends. New responsibilities. New mistakes. New wins. Some days they cooked for the first time. Other days they forgot to eat. They learnt things textbooks couldn't teach; about roommates, fixing broken taps, crashing bikes, fixing broken spirits. That's life, I guess.

And as I sat there, clapping as their names were called out, I wasn't just thinking about them. I thought of my own friends. The ones I made when I didn't know where my own "library" was in life. Some stayed. Some faded. But all shaped something in me.

They say now comes the real world. Jobs. Meetings. Projects. Salaries. Targets. But I think the real world began the moment they left home and had to figure out dinner. And now? Now they'll learn how to stay steady when things don't go their way. How to do what needs to be done, even when no one's watching. That's the stuff that matters. Not the grades. Not the paychecks. Just showing up. Doing right. Staying true.

So yeah, today wasn't just their convocation. It was mine, in some small way. A graduation of my thoughts. A look back. A quiet smile forward.

And the best part? They now have friends who saw them through these five years. That matters more than they know. Maybe more than they'll ever say.

Here's to moving ahead. One real day at a time

Ramblings & the Relentless Tick of Time

"If I had to sum up life in three words, it's this: It goes on."

I've read that quote before, but today it stayed with me a little longer. I kept thinking about what it really means-not just for me or people I know, but for life in general. For the world. For time itself.

Life doesn't just go on for us, it has always gone on. Long before we were born. Long after we'll be gone. The Earth has been spinning for millions of years. People came, people went. Animals, empires, languages, kings. All of them had their time. And still, life moved on. Not slowly, not quickly; just at its own pace.

So where do we fit in?

Our lives are short, really. Some live 80, some 50, some even less. We chase so many things. We worry about getting older. We try to freeze timc in photos, in achievements, in stories. But no matter what we do, the clock keeps ticking.

And maybe that's the strange beauty of it. That we matter and don't matter at the same time.

When we're hurting, this thought can help:

No pain lasts forever. The world doesn't stop because we've fallen. Sooner or later, something changes. The weight becomes lighter. We move again. When we're happy, this thought can remind us: Don't take it for granted. Enjoy it. Nothing stays the same.

Yet then another thought wandered in: Even a train stops at a destination. It starts from one too. So what about life? Are we just rolling endlessly, or are there pauses, stations, departures, and arrivals that matter?

Maybe life does go on, but it's not a straight line. Maybe it's a series of stops. Sometimes we board new phases, sometimes we disembark from old ones. Some people get off too early. Some miss their train. Some sit in the wrong coach for too long, staring out of windows that don't show them anything they care about. And then there's us - carrying our luggage, trying to find a seat, occasionally losing our ticket, occasionally helping someone find theirs.

Maybe that's the nuance the quote skips over.

That "it goes on" doesn't mean endlessly, blindly, relentlessly. It means we move. We adapt. We grieve and grow. We leave, and we arrive. And even when life halts, when it really feels like everything's come to a stop, it's just the engine catching its breath before the next stretch.

So maybe the more accurate quote would be:

It goes on, with stops. But who am I to rewrite someone else's wisdom? Still, I like my version better today. Because it gives me space to pause without guilt. To stand at the platform. To let people go. To wait for the next train. Or maybe just sit quietly with a cup of hot chocolate, and breathe.

Because yes, it goes on.

With or without us

Ramblings After a Velumani Kind of Day

We had a session today with Dr. A. Velumani. A man who built a business from ₹500 in his pocket to a multi-thousand-crore empire. But you'd never guess it listening to him. No expensive suit, no slides, no jargon. Just raw truths, wrapped in wit from a man who lives frugal and travelled economy class.

One line stuck:

"Humans celebrate the past but fear the future."

It got me thinking about my parents. They've reached a stage where every plan that gets cancelled hits deeper. We kids keep saying "next time," thinking time stretches endlessly. They, on the other hand, live with a quiet urgency. They don't say it, but you can feel it-in the way they ask when you're visiting, in how they prepare for your arrival weeks in advance.

Velumani spoke of focus-how the world is full of noise, and unless you tune in, you'll keep drifting.

He spoke of frugality-how he made every rupee count, not just in business but in life.

He said peace is underrated-that too much ambition with too little silence leads to restlessness, not success.

He didn't just talk about building wealth-he spoke of companionship, of staying grounded, of knowing who walks with you when the spotlight is off.

One powerful line:

"Success needs hunger, not thirst."

It made sense. Hunger drives you to work. Thirst pushes you to show off. There's a difference.

What stood out most was how little he spoke about money, despite having so much of it. For someone whose net worth could fill headlines, he talked more about life, love, purpose, peace.

And somehow, it all came back to the same thought: we're all racing, but we don't know when the race ends. So, maybe slow down once in a while. Call home. Book the ticket. Make time-not excuses.

Just some thoughts. Nothing new maybe. But from a man who started with ₹500, I was reminded again-value isn't always in currency. Sometimes, it's in the people we show up for

The Power of Talking

Talk.

Just talk.

To your children, your parents, your friends.

I don't know when the world changed so much. Everything's faster, more scattered. We're always connected - yet rarely connecting. Everyone's chasing something, but conversations... they're falling behind.

I often think back to our days growing up in a joint family. In our Bohra household, we ate in a thaal; that big round metal plate, placed on a low stand called a chumli or kunli. Eight of us, sometimes more, would sit cross-legged around it.

The meal always started with Bismillah and a pinch of salt. And the golden rule? Conversations around the thaal had to be light-hearted, respectful, and pleasant. No serious topics, no complaints, no harsh words; nothing that would make anyone lose their appetite or feel uncomfortable. It was about sharing, not just food, but warmth. Laughter. Teasing. Small joys.

That thaal was more than a plate - it was the heart of the home. The patriarch would guide the talk with wisdom or wit. The matriarch, always alert, would be serving with care - knowing who liked what, remembering everyone's little quirks. It was a place where food brought people together, and words kept them close.

Fast forward to today - we live across continents. Kids go abroad to study and often stay on. Parents remain in their hometowns, holding on to memories and checking phones for that one awaited call. Friends disappear into work, meetings, routines. My parents wait for a call. So do I; from my children. And so, I've made it a practice to speak to them at least once a day. Not because there's something urgent. But because there's love. And that's enough.

Talking is healing.

It's a free therapy, a daily grounding.

Friends keep you young. Their voices remind you who you used to be - and still are, somewhere beneath the layers of age and responsibility.

Kids may not understand this yet.

But one day they will - when they find themselves on the other side of a quiet room, waiting for a phone to ring.

So here's my little reminder - Keep talking.

Before memories turn to messages.

Before time turns those voices into echoes.

Before silence settles where laughter once lived.

*Some conversations feed the soul more than the food feeds the stomach.

And sometimes, all it takes is a pinch of salt and a little time.*

Summa Cum Laude - But That's Not the Whole Story

It's graduation season. There's something magical in the air-caps flying, proud smiles, eyes glistening behind phone cameras trying to freeze a moment that took years to build. When we saw Summa Cum Laude written next to the names of our two boys, it was a moment of quiet pride. Not for the title alone, but for everything behind it-the years of late nights, the moments of self-doubt, the deadlines, the distance, and the discipline.

But truth be told, not every child walks up with medals. And not every proud parent hears their child's name followed by academic honors. Yet, that doesn't take away from the real success that often goes unseen. Success sometimes comes dressed in awards and applause, and other times it comes quietly-in the form of resilience, recovery, and simply not giving up.

We've seen kids who had all the resources but struggled to find motivation, and others who came from less but fought their way through with grit alone. We've seen brilliance that couldn't always be measured by grades and courage that never made it to a certificate. And as parents, we've come to realize-our job isn't to compare but to stand by them, to guide when needed, and to simply believe when they stop believing in themselves.

For children, life after graduation is just beginning. The world beyond the classroom will care less about titles and more about effort, attitude, and how you handle failure. Be kind. Stay curious. Call home once in a while. And remember, your degrees may open doors, but your values will decide which rooms you belong in.

For parents, this is a moment to pause. To feel proud not just of their success but of your role in the journey-the sacrifices, the silent prayers, the firm advice, and the patient listening. We often carry their stress as our own, hoping they'll rise, worrying when they fall. But in the end, what matters most is that they grew, and you stood by them through it all.

Yes, Summa Cum Laude is a beautiful line on a certificate. But the real reward is watching them become capable, compassionate human beings. That's a distinction no paper can capture.

So while we celebrate the success of our boys, we also celebrate every child who made it through, every parent who held on through the ups and downs, and every family that turned effort into achievement-quietly, patiently, and with all their heart

Mangoes, Madness & Memories

Today, I called three of my childhood friends. Friends I grew up with. Since the age of four, till I was eighteen. Then life happened - we moved houses, got busy with studies, careers, deadlines, and distance. But somehow, the connection stayed - through occasional messages, voice notes, and calls like today.

We started talking, and soon we were back in those summer afternoons - when green mangoes were our prized possessions. We'd pluck them (without permission, of course), divide them, sometimes argue over them, but always end up sharing. Someone mentioned how of the eight trees in our compound, only three remain. The rest either fell on their own or were brought down. And then someone quietly said - "Even the people from that time are like those trees… some gone to paradise, some still around… just older now."

It hit me. Hard.

From there, we went on to talk about the plays and dramas we used to perform in our house - we used to print handmade tickets, charge the neighbourhood kids 10 paise, and dress up in household clothes with holes in them, calling it "costume." The bathroom towel became a royal cloak, and the bindi made with a red / black sketch pen made us warriors or kings, depending on the role.

And oh, the games of hide and seek! The boys always ganged up to make me "denner," and I'd always end up being punished. I used to hate playing with them for that very reason - but now, when we laughed about it today, I realised even the unfairness was part of the fun.

Then there was that day - I broke my piggy bank to buy Krustom Ice Creams for my friends. Felt like a king that day, till I got a solid pasting from mom and was locked up in the lavatory for hours. That story, my friends still remember and laugh at - more than I do.

Swimming classes at Shivaji Park pool, movies in the single screens, school tantrums, community festivals where we'd all wear matching outfits sewn by someone's aunty - it all came rushing back. So many simple joys, so many memories packed in narrow lanes and even narrower pockets.

We also remembered the elders of that time - some of whom I was terrified of, and some I adored. They were part of our lives, always around. They taught us, scolded us, fed us, and inspired us - without ever trying too hard.

And then, my grandfather. Everyone had something nice to say about him. He lived a simple life, but with dignity. He used to say in Gujarati, "Namein te sav ne gamein."

Which means - "The one who bows and stays humble is liked by all."

He used to tell us - Do such deeds that people speak good of you behind your back and remember you kindly when you are no more. And when he passed away, that's exactly what happened. People came from far and wide… to pay respects, to share stories, to talk about how he touched their lives.

Today's call was not just a reunion of friends - it was a gentle reminder. That the best memories are made from the simplest things. That people matter more than possessions. That laughter over green mangoes and 10-paise tickets is worth more than all the subscriptions and streaming apps in the world.

And that while time may pull down the mango trees and take away some people... memories, if we keep them alive, will always be our shade.

Back to Class 5: Autobiography of an Old Wall Clock

Nostalgia hit me today. The kind that makes you smell chalk, hear the school bell, and remember the rustle of notebooks in your brown school bag.

Remember those essays we were always asked to write?

"Autobiography of a pen."

"Autobiography of a shoe."

Or the classic… "Autobiography of a wall clock."

And so, I thought, let me relive that memory. I imagined myself back in my Class 5 classroom in my convent school uniform, trying to finish the essay before the bell rang. Here's what I would've written then, in all innocence:

Autobiography of an Old Wall Clock

What are you staring at?

Yes, I'm that same old wall clock. The one who once ruled the living room wall, right above the TV - proud, loud, and always on time.

I woke everyone up, sent kids to school, reminded mummy to switch off the gas, and papa to leave for work. Even the cat knew when it was lunch, thanks to me!

Tick-tick, I worked day and night; no Sundays, no holidays. But one day, I got tired. My hands slowed down. My tick faded. They tried fixing me, but soon, a shiny new clock took my place.

Now, I lie quietly in the store room, behind some boxes. Forgotten. But still listening. Still remembering.

You may think I'm useless now, but I've seen years pass, families grow, and stories unfold. I may not tick anymore, but my time was full of moments.

And now, the lesson…

Just like that clock, there are people in our lives who kept things going; without fuss, without praise. And when they slow down or step aside, we often forget their time, their effort, their quiet presence.

This little essay isn't just about a wall clock. It's about parents, grandparents, teachers, loyal friends, and silent helpers. The ones who may no longer "tick" in the center of our lives, but whose impact was timeless.

So maybe, just maybe today remember someone from your past who helped you move forward.

Because even when the hands stop moving, the memories don't

Of Climates, Characters, and Countries

Yesterday, we were discussing something seemingly simple, yet as we went on, it unfolded into layers more intricate than we had imagined-Does the nature of people depend on the climate they live in?

A question that sounds almost poetic, but as we dug deeper, we found more questions waiting, like matryoshka dolls-one inside the other.

Think about it.

Is it the scorching sun that breeds hot tempers? The biting cold that chisels out stoic faces? Is it the tropical breeze that makes people more easy-going? Or is it all just romantic nonsense we tell ourselves to make sense of things we cannot explain?

Yet when you travel across nations, you do observe patterns. Some people are loud, expressive, passionate, quick to react. Some are reserved, cautious, composed. Some are painfully polite. Some, blunt to the point of being brash. Some celebrate in the streets at the smallest of joys, others internalise happiness like a well-guarded treasure.

Now, of course, we don't mean to generalise. But every nation, like every home, carries an aroma-a temperament-that you can sense the moment you step in. And one begins to wonder-is it the climate? Or the centuries of culture shaped by that climate? Or is it governance? The invisible hand of leadership that either lifts or crushes the soul of a people?

Take a war-torn country. It doesn't matter what their weather is. The clouds are heavy not because of monsoons, but from smoke, suspicion, and sorrow. Generations grow up learning survival, not serenity. And this seeps into how people speak, behave, trust-or don't.

Then you see a country where policies are made keeping in mind the child born on the street as much as the one born in a mansion. Where the weakest has a voice and the strongest has ears. Where envy is replaced by empathy. Where success is not a zero-sum game.

Here, the people smile easily. Stand in queues without pushing. Respect the elderly without laws forcing them to. Here, the happiness index isn't just a number in a UN report-it's in how strangers hold doors for each other. How a forgotten wallet is returned intact. How you sleep without checking the lock thrice.

So maybe it's not just the climate, but the collective climate of the mind and soul. A home where children are raised to share, to question, to be kind. A society that teaches pride without prejudice. Leaders who remember they are servants first. Laws that uphold dignity more than control. Media that informs, not incites. And people who don't hoard but help.

When there is no need to prove you are better than your neighbour, when weakness is not mocked but supported, when success isn't flaunted but celebrated silently-then peace comes naturally. And slowly, almost magically, the internal weather changes. From storms of restlessness to skies of contentment.

Maybe, in such a world, the cold won't make people cold. Nor will the heat make them harsh.

Because the real temperature is not outside.

It's within

Of Clowns, Circuses, and Channels

A dear friend posted on his whatsapp status:

"Don't blame the clown for being a clown. Ask yourself why you keep going to the circus."

At first, I smiled. But the more I thought about it, the more I realized how often this applies to our lives.

Years ago, I worked with someone in a senior position-loud, flamboyant, and constantly stirring drama in meetings. Every conversation was a performance. Decisions delayed, egos stroked, and truth often buried under theatrics. Everyone complained about him behind closed doors. Yet every week, like clockwork, we'd all attend his "Monday morning shows", hoping maybe this time he'd be different.

He never changed. Why would he? We kept showing up.

Eventually, I stopped reacting. I would prepare, speak up when needed, and leave the drama behind. The moment I stopped being part of the audience, I stopped being part of the problem.

It's the same with today's media.

We criticize news channels for their bias, their noise, their drama. But we keep watching. We let them enter our homes, hijack our dining tables, fuel our fears.

They show what sells. And what sells... is us.

Whether it's in offices, families, friend circles, or national media-clowns thrive because we let the circus continue.

Real change won't come from shouting at the stage. It'll come when we quietly stop attending shows that add no value to our minds or lives.

Not every drama needs a reaction.

Not every performance needs an audience.

And not every clown deserves our time.

Sometimes, the wisest thing you can do-for your peace, for your values, and for society-is to get up, fold your arms… and walk out of the tent

"Maalesh – A Pause Worth Taking"

This evening, in the most ordinary of places-the parking lot outside my gym in Jabriya-I witnessed something quietly powerful.

A car was trying to reverse out of a tight space. Maybe the driver was adjusting the seat, maybe his mind was somewhere else, or maybe he was just being careful. But the driver waiting behind him wasn't in a patient mood. He started honking, again and again. You could see the frustration building. Impatience had taken the wheel.

Then something unexpected happened.

The driver trying to exit stepped out of his car and walked toward the honking one. For a moment, I thought it would escalate. A typical parking lot showdown, maybe some yelling, hand gestures, the usual.

But then… recognition.

They knew each other.

Smiles appeared. Hands were shaken. Cheeks kissed, the familiar Arab greeting. A laugh or two, followed by a cheerful "Maalesh."

(Maalesh-a common Arabic expression loosely meaning "It's okay," "No problem," or "Let it go." A single word that dissolves tension and invites understanding.)

And just like that, what began as a moment of irritation turned into a warm reunion between two friends.

It made me pause.

What if we always assumed the person on the other side of our frustration was a friend? Someone we knew? Someone we once shared a meal or a moment with?

Most of our everyday anger doesn't come from serious offenses. It comes from seconds lost, delays we didn't expect, people not moving at our pace. But if we paused, just for a breath, and imagined the other person as someone familiar-a cousin, a neighbour, a colleague from the past-would our response change?

Why does it take familiarity to unlock our patience?

"Maalesh" is more than a word. It's a reset button. It reminds us that not everything needs a reaction, that not every delay is an insult, and that sometimes, letting go is the better choice.

In a world constantly rushing, we forget how quickly things can shift when we bring a little humanity into the moment. That parking lot scene could've ended in anger. Instead, it ended in laughter.

All it took was a face they recognized-and a choice to respond with warmth.

Next time, before the honk, maybe we can all try the pause. And who knows? Maybe that stranger in front of us is just a forgotten friend

Forwarded Many Times, Understood Very Little

They say perception is the lowest form of knowledge. And the more I see of the world today, the more I believe it. Everyone seems to know everything, based on half a reel, a cropped screenshot, a 30-second clip, or something forwarded 16 times with a "forwarded many times" label still proudly attached.

We grew up in a time when "knowing" meant reading, asking questions, failing at it, asking again, and eventually forming an opinion after a few scratches and bruises. Today, opinions are formed first and facts are hunted later-only to reinforce what we already believed. And if the facts don't match? Well, we switch the source, not the stance.

I remember as kids, our elders would say, "Don't judge until you hear both sides." Today, both sides are yelling at once, and we pick the louder one. Somewhere along the way, we confused noise with truth.

So, who's responsible for this mess? The media? Schools? Social platforms? Influencers who talk fast and read slow? Or us-for becoming lazy consumers of packaged thinking?

Honestly, it's all of the above. And maybe none of them. Maybe it's the pace. Maybe it's convenience. Maybe it's the constant craving for dopamine disguised as "being updated."

How do we handle this? Maybe we slow down. Maybe we ask, "How do you know this?" before forwarding or reacting. Maybe we start rewarding people for saying "I'm not sure" rather than pretending to know everything.

There's no quick fix. But maybe the next time someone says, "Everyone is saying this," we pause and ask, "Who exactly is everyone?"

Because perception may be the starting point but staying there is a choice.

I'd rather be questioned for thinking than applauded for assuming

The Secret Gender Bias of Animal Sayings!

Ever wondered why most Hindi (and even English) proverbs that talk about animals almost always mention male animals? Why is it always ullu ka pattha (son of an owl), gadhe ka baccha (son of a donkey), kawwa chale hans ki chaal (crow tries to walk like a swan), and never the daughter?

Let's take a look:

"Ullu ka pattha" (son of an owl) – Ironically used to call someone foolish, though owls are known for wisdom.

"Gadhe ka baccha" (donkey's son) – A classic insult. No one ever blames the gadhi.

"Kawwa chale hans ki chaal" (crow tries to walk like a swan) – Poking fun at someone trying to copy others and failing.

"Aa bail mujhe maar" (Come, oh bull, hit me) – Calling trouble upon yourself.

"Bandar kya jaane adrak ka swaad (What does a monkey know of ginger's taste) – Someone who doesn't understand value or quality.

"Jab chuhe ki maut aati hai, toh woh sher ki taraf bhaagta hai" (When a mouse's death nears, it runs towards the lion) – Refers to reckless bravery when one is doomed anyway.

"Oonth ke mooh mein jeera" (Cumin seed in a camel's mouth) – Too little for someone or something very big.

And interestingly, in all these - the animal is male.

No mention of daughters or females in any of these sayings. Coincidence? Or some secret agreement among early proverb-makers?

Even English has the same trend:

"Stubborn as a mule" – Blamed for being difficult.

"Strong as an ox" – Praised for power.

"Let the cat out of the bag" – Accused of spilling secrets.

Again - male references everywhere.

But let's be clear - this is just a fun reflection on language and expressions. In real life, women are not just present - they lead, they pioneer, and they elevate. From homes to boardrooms, from labs to leadership, from silent strength to outspoken brilliance - they are the backbone of families and the face of change. There's no comparison in proverbs or positions - because in the real world, they don't follow the path, they make it.

Until next Note -

Let's enjoy our idioms, laugh at our language quirks, and remember that behind every wise saying, there's often an even wiser woman not mentioned in it.

Random Rambling and Rumination

(Because sometimes, over green tea and daily wanderings, these thoughts just show up uninvited - like the owl in our idioms.)

"What you Resist, Perceives. What you Accept, Dissolves."

I've often found that life's trickiest problems have a strange way of behaving like uninvited guests. The more you resist them, the longer they stay - stubbornly sipping your time, energy, and peace. But the moment you say, "Alright, I see you. Sit if you must," something unexpected happens - they lose their power.

Think about it. A corporate crisis, a tough client, an internal conflict, or even a personal mistake - when we stiffen up and fight them, they loom larger. They steal our sleep, drive meetings into overtime, and cloud our judgment. But when we face them with calm acceptance - not defeat, not indifference, but simple acknowledgment - they begin to shrink. Solutions appear. Conversations soften. Opportunities sneak back into the room.

In boardrooms and brainstorming sessions, I've seen the same principle at play. Teams that spend more energy denying a problem or finding someone to blame, only end up building castles around the issue. Meanwhile, teams that say, "Yes, there is a problem. Let's look at it together," almost always find a way through.

Acceptance isn't about giving up. It's about loosening the grip of fear. It's about making space for clarity and common sense. When you stop wrestling with reality, you free your hands to build something better.

Even in our personal lives, small annoyances - a colleague's stubbornness, a family member's habits, even our own failures

- behave like shadows. Chase them, and they chase you back. Shine the light of acceptance, and they quietly fall away.

And if ever you feel you're off track, remember - there are no fixed tracks.

In the ebb and flow of work and life, we are not robots. We are not designed to be perfect. Let imperfections creep in. Notice them, accept them - but don't let them define you.

Today's world - spinning faster than ever - would do well to remember this. Corporates, nations, individuals - we all tend to fight the winds of change, the truths we don't like, the faults we don't want to admit. But real strength lies not in resistance, but in wise acceptance. Only then can we dissolve barriers, heal wounds, and move forward.

Sometimes, the best way to win the battle is to stop fighting it.

And so, I remind myself - and anyone willing to listen - next time a storm brews, don't tighten your sails in panic. Pause. Listen. Let the wind pass through you. It might just carry you somewhere better.

"When the Guest Becomes the Host"

Day before yesterday, at a conference packed with discussions, business suits, and the usual flurry of agendas, I heard something simple-yet it stayed with me far longer than any keynote speech.

A respected Kuwaiti gentleman, an elder statesman of sorts, was asked to say a few words and he said with quiet pride:

"If you visit us as guests, you will find that our welcome will be such that you will feel we are the guests, and you are the home."

No slides. No jargon. Just truth. And I couldn't help but nod. Because over the years, time and again, I've experienced this hospitality-not as a courtesy, but as a way of life here. Whether it's a cup of gahwa served with quiet warmth, or the insistence on sharing a meal even if it's the last morsel left at home, there's a certain simplicity in the Kuwaiti way of hosting that doesn't need decoration. In fact, there's an old Kuwaiti saying I once heard from an elderly gentleman in Souq Mubarakiya:

"El bayt baytak, hatta law ma fee 'inda illa finjan gahwa."

(This house is your house, even if all I have is a cup of coffee.)

Another one goes:

"El deewaniya ma tesakker illa 'ala daifha."

(The deewaniya does not close until the guest leaves.)

And not out of formality, but out of pure feeling.

Sometimes, in this world of networking dinners and business meet-ups, we forget that real bonds are built not over LinkedIn connections, but over late-night gahva, warm bread, and stories shared in courtyards under the desert moon. This land may be known for oil and skyscrapers, but its soul still resides in old deewaniyas, palm tree shadows, and elders who still remember what it meant to serve dates to travelers and strangers.

One of my Kuwaiti friends once told me:

"We don't count the guests we host; we remember the stories they left behind."

It's true. Here, hospitality isn't scheduled. It flows. Unforced, unfiltered. Sometimes with silence. Sometimes with song. And maybe that's a lesson for all of us in our fast-moving lives. That respect doesn't come from rituals. It comes from making someone feel that they belong.

Even when they don't speak your language.

Even when they come from a different land.

Even when they carry nothing but their presence.

I left that conference with a stronger conviction:

In a world obsessed with self-promotion, there's quiet dignity in treating a guest like royalty-and making them forget they were ever outsiders.

And in that moment, you become more than a host.

You become family

Buffet of Emotions

Yesterday's lunch was at Five Star Hotel - a buffet gathering hosted by a dear friend. His parents were visiting, his son is about to leave for university, and it was also his birthday yesterday. A house full of emotions-celebration, pride, nostalgia, and a quiet sense of time moving on.

While the buffet had something for everyone, I kept it simple-my usual salad and a few grills. But what truly filled us was the warmth in the room. Watching the grandparents beam with pride, and the parents balancing joy with the silent ache of seeing their child fly out of the nest, I couldn't help but drift into my own memories.

It feels like just yesterday when we dropped our children off to pursue their studies. And now, this month, they complete their course. Four years-gone in the blink of an eye. We missed them deeply-missed the mess, the noise, the comfort of having them around. I know they missed us too-missed Kuwait, missed home, missed the feeling of being completely understood.

Now, they step into the next phase-jobs, startups, maybe more studies, maybe finding love, maybe chasing a dream we haven't even imagined yet. We don't know where destiny will take them.

Being parents from the subcontinent, our dreams stretch a bit further-we think of weddings, grandchildren, and a settled life. But even beyond those dreams, what we really wish for is a life that's simple, kind, and fulfilling.

That's the cycle of life.

All we really pray for is a humble, simple, modest, happy, and fulfilling life. Because success looks different to everyone. But peace, kindness, and contentment? That's what we all really want. A good life-for them, and through them, for us

What we are, we are.

She laughed as she said it-"I've always been this talkative since school days!"

And then, almost proudly, she told me how her teachers would make her kneel in the corridor with hands up because she just couldn't keep quiet. Her classmates finished lessons; she finished stories. That childhood trait? It's still with her. She owns it, flaunts it even.

And it got me thinking-

Are we really wired a certain way from the start? And if so, can we truly change?

People grow, learn, mature, adapt. But something about that basic nature-our default setting-seems to stay. Like a song that plays in the background no matter what playlist you switch to.

You see it when the richest man in the room, wearing a crisp suit and throwing around jargon, runs into an old school buddy and suddenly bursts into carefree laughter, talking in his native slang. Or when the most serious, silent office colleague is seen giggling uncontrollably with her childhood friend at a café. The polished adult pauses for a bit, and the real kid shows up.

Maybe our upbringing, education, and life experiences shape our choices and sharpen our rough edges. But the core? It usually sticks around.

Of course, life teaches us to tone things down. We learn what to say, when to speak, and who's watching. But the essence peeks through in unguarded moments. Like that talkative girl-who now runs meetings, narrates stories, connects effortlessly-still chirpy, still her.

Maybe change isn't about flipping the switch. Maybe it's just learning how to live with who we are-without disturbing the neighbourhood. Because in the end, what we are, we are.

And maybe that's not something to fix-maybe that's something to honour.

Once You Carry Your Own Water…

"Once you carry your own water, you will realise the value of every drop."

Read that somewhere, and it hit home harder than expected. It reminded me of an old Reader's Digest piece-those short, powerful anecdotes that stuck with you longer than any self-help book. In that one, a father visits his grown-up son, now proud owner of a swanky new house. The father walks in, looks around, and calmly switches on all the lights, fans, maybe even the AC. The son, startled, quickly says, "Dad! What are you doing? Electricity's expensive!" The father just smiles and says, "This is exactly what I used to tell you when you were young."

That line-simple, soft, but loaded.

There's a strange kind of silence that falls on you when you hear your own words coming from your kid's mouth-or when you react exactly like your parents once did, even though you swore you never would.

You grow up thinking they're just being fussy or old-fashioned. And then life flips the script. The day your salary is on the line, the day you're the one buying groceries, worrying about bills, staying up at night because your child has a fever and won't sleep-you finally understand. No lectures. No sermons. Just… quiet understanding.

I think that's the biggest plot twist in life. You spend years rolling your eyes at your parents' concerns, only to realize one day-you've become them. And it's not a bad thing. It's not karma.

It's just… life. Full circle. You now know why they used to knock on your bathroom door shouting, "You're wasting water!" or switch off lights in empty rooms like they were paid per bulb.

Parenting is mostly thankless. It's not glamorous. There's no standing ovation for the 2 a.m. diaper changes or the silent sacrifices. But then one day, your child tells their kid the same thing you once told them. That's your standing ovation. Quiet, but deep. You smile. You've done something right.

So yes, once you carry your own water, you will realise the value of every drop. Once you pay your own electricity bill, you'll remember why your dad always switched off that fan. And once you become a parent, you'll realize how much your parents truly gave-even when they said nothing at all.

I think that's the curve of life. You start off thinking your parents are from another planet. Then one fine day, without warning, you look in the mirror-and there they are. In your words. In your worries. In your way of folding the laundry.

It's humbling. It's grounding. And strangely, it's comforting.

Because that's when you truly understand what love without conditions looks like

Just as is

Woke up today wondering why every day insists on starting so early. The sun doesn't ask for permission, the alarm doesn't care if you slept late, and somehow, the toothbrush is always missing just when you need it.

Started with a celery and green apple smoothie, which sounds healthier than it tastes. Followed by my usual black coffee in the office-strong, bitter, loyal.

There's a mug in the pantry that reads "Mondays should be optional." But today's Wednesday, and I still agree.

Had coffee twice before 11 am. That's either productivity or addiction, and I'm not ready to pick sides. Also, I've now started judging people based on how they hold their mugs. Pinky up? Suspicious. Two-handed grip? Respect.

Someone in office asked if Excel could feel emotions. Judging by the way it crashes when you're on a deadline, I think it feels spite. Not to blame excel fully. the power surge today made excel cry.

A Spilopelia senegalensis-yes, the local laughing dove-stared at me for five minutes on the window ledge. I stared back. I think I blinked first. The bird wins.

The Kuwait Times had 2 pages of politics, 2 on medicinal impact of Uncle Sam's tariff, 2 of celebrities and sports, and 0.5 of common sense.

Also, how come nobody ever finishes a pen? They just disappear. Like socks. And good ideas mid-shower.

While returning home, at the 3rd RR signal which seems to turn red faster than the speed at which i gulp a coke, I saw a toddler trying to unlock his mom's phone with facial recognition and failing. He looked hurt. The phone didn't recognize him, but his chocolate-stained fingers definitely left a mark on the windowpane.

Sometimes, it's okay to write for no reason. Not every page needs to make sense. Some just need to exist. Like that drawer we all have with batteries, keys that unlock nothing, and an old Nokia charger.

Anyway, if you've read this far, thank you for doing absolutely nothing productive for the last two minutes.

"If You Learn How to Die, You Learn How to Live."

That line hit me like a quiet whisper in a crowded room. Morrie's words to Mitch weren't philosophical fluff - they were plain, simple, and real. They stop you for a moment, make you put your phone down, shut out the background noise, and just think.

We live as if we're going to be around forever - rushing to meet deadlines, chasing after titles, checking off bucket lists. We argue over petty things, hoard what we don't need, and forget to smile at strangers. But the moment you truly realize you're not here forever, something shifts. You start looking at life differently.

You breathe slower. You hug longer. You speak gentler.

When you accept the truth of death - not in fear, but in awareness - you start choosing how to live. You stop being in a hurry. You listen more. You stop needing to win every argument. You start being.

In the noise of the world - politics, opinions, wars, likes, shares - what really matters gets lost. We don't need louder voices; we need calmer minds. We need fewer followers and more friendships.

We live better when we let go of the need to control everything. After all, it is not us who decide when the curtain falls. We are not the conductor. We are part of the music, but not the composer.

Maybe life isn't about doing more, but doing right.

Living kindly.

Leaving quietly.

Loving truly.

And above all, living with humility. The kind that says - I don't have all the answers. I never did. But I'm learning.

One day at a time.

One breath at a time.

Until He calls us home

(Tuesdays with Morrie)

Silent Thunder

The loudest word ever shouted is probably the word 'quiet'. Funny how life moves. The things meant to calm us often arrive with force, and the things meant to shake us sometimes whisper.

Wars are fought to bring peace. We rush so we can relax later. We plan for the future while ignoring the moment right in front of us. We stay awake reading about rest and wake up feeling anything but rested.

Life is packed with these little contradictions we bump into every day.

We save our favourite clothes for a special day, forgetting that an ordinary midweek morning might need that small spark more than any celebration. We give kind words to everyone around us, yet speak to ourselves and our dear ones like we're our own worst critic. We carry power banks everywhere, but walk around mentally flat. We claim we don't have time for those who matter, yet somehow have time for everything that doesn't.

And then came the pandemic, quietly teaching a few lessons that should've been obvious.

We learnt that savings matter, but hoarding life does not. That being wise with money is good, but being a miser steals the joy from the very life we're trying to secure. That buying something expensive only to gift others while denying ourselves basic joys is its own strange imbalance. That life is meant to be lived - sensibly, yes, but also wholeheartedly.

We learnt that a simple home-cooked meal can feel richer than any restaurant. That long walks with family can outshine the most luxurious trips. That health, time, and memories don't care about bank balances.

Maybe the point isn't to resolve these contradictions, but to acknowledge them. To smile at their odd timing. To live with a bit of balance - to save, but not shrink; to spend, but not show off; to be cautious, but not fearful.

When we understand that life runs on these mismatched truths, we stop chasing perfection and start living with intention.

Let things settle a bit. What stays is usually what matters

The RSVP Tug-of-War Diaries

FOMO vs JOMO has become the modern tug of war. One side pulling you towards every party, every panel talk, every brunch-that-looks-better-on-Instagram-than-in-real-life. The other side quietly whispering, "Boss, stay home... your sofa is also a loyal friend."

Last weekend, I watched a friend sprint from one event to another like he had signed a secret contract with the universe - 'thou shall not miss any selfie opportunity'. By the time he reached his third gathering, even his smile had resigned. Meanwhile another friend cancelled everything, sat at home with a cup of chai and proudly announced, "Today I'm practising JOMO." He said it with the same pride as someone saying they completed a marathon. Honestly, in today's world, choosing to stay out of the noise is a marathon.

This is page-3 life in nutshell. One person updates stories every seven minutes. Another turns the phone face down, as if it emits radiation. Some feel restless if they aren't tagged in at least one event a week. Some get peace knowing no one even knows where they are.

But here's the funny thing. Both groups think the other is missing something.

Truth is, we all live in this constant circus of wanting to be everywhere and nowhere at the same time. We chase invitations as if attendance is the new currency of relevance. We pretend we enjoy the noise even when the soul secretly wants silence. And then we wonder why Monday feels heavy.

Somewhere between FOMO and JOMO lies the real sweet spot: choosing where you add value and where you simply drain your battery. Not every room needs you. Not every gathering deserves your bandwidth. And not every face needs a forced smile.

The message, if any, is this: show up where your presence matters, not where your absence will be noticed. That's the real freedom. That's the real joy. And that's how you keep your peace without losing your humour in this mad, competitive, selfie-driven world

Time, Not Distance

Yesterday's chat with my very close friend and bestie began as a casual talk about how long it takes to get from one place to another. In smaller towns of India, a 5–8 km ride is nothing. Ten minutes after dinner, fifteen during the day - and you're there. Simple.

But then we laughed, remembering our Mumbai days. There, distance was never measured in kilometres. It was measured in time. "Twenty minutes by train." "Forty-five by bus." "Half an hour by auto if the driver's in a good mood."

I don't think I even knew how far my college was in kilometres. All I knew was: leave home at 7:42 to catch the 7:49 local, else I'd be late for the 8:30 lecture. Life in Mumbai was timed to the minute, not mapped by distance

Then came Kuwait, where I finally learned the concept of kilometres where the first question isn't how long, but how far . Here, 10 km is simply 10 km. The roads flow, time obeys, and everything somehow moves in sync. It's the exact opposite of Mumbai - there, you guessed the time and hoped the distance matched; here, you know the distance and trust the time will.

I realised, cities teach us how we measure life itself. In big metros, we lose kilometres to congestion and patience to deadlines. We stop noticing how the world moves while we stay glued. Maybe that's why time feels shorter there, we've already spent most of it waiting at traffic lights.

But somewhere between these two worlds, a thought hit me - life too can be seen this way. In our younger days, we measure everything by time - how fast we can reach, how quickly we can succeed, how soon we can prove ourselves. Later, we begin to notice the distance we've actually covered - the people we met, the pauses that shaped us, the detours that changed our course.

Perhaps that's the quiet beauty of life - we're all travelling somewhere, but it's not just about reaching. Some roads are meant to slow us down, some teach us patience, and some remind us that time is only a measure - it's the journey that makes it meaningful.

We ended our call smiling - two Mumbaikars, once chasing time, now finally learning to enjoy the distance

Some of the People, Some of the Time

You can please some people at all times and all people at some times, but never all people at all times. Borrowed from what's often linked to Abraham Lincoln's line on fooling people, this one seems to echo through every corridor of life - from home to office, from gatherings to WhatsApp groups.

Look around and you'll see it everywhere. Try hosting a family dinner - someone will find the biryani too spicy, someone else will say it's bland, and one soul will ask why there's no sugar-free dessert. Organize a community event and you'll know what true diplomacy means. The seating arrangement becomes a political science experiment - where egos clash, importance takes center stage, and being seen in the "right row" matters more than the purpose of the evening. Someone will insist their chair be moved just a little forward, another will wonder why they weren't called on stage, and a few will quietly calculate whose name was mentioned more in the vote of thanks.

In projects, it's no different. You try to please the owner, the owner's representative, the contractor, and the consultant - but seldom are all happy at the same time. It's rare that the plans, designs, construction progress, financials, and payments all move in perfect sync and reach the finish line with everyone smiling. Someone's always waiting for a variation order, another is chasing certification, and one more is questioning the design change.

Even offices aren't spared. Announce bonuses or raises and watch the smiles fade faster than the ink dries. The joy lasts until someone whispers, "But why did they get more?" The human mind has this natural tendency to compare - a bit like in exams, where one examiner writes "excellent" and another writes "needs clarity" for the same answer. Satisfaction, it seems, is always graded differently.

Life, really, is a full-time lesson in learning that there's no one-size-fits-all. People come in different shapes, moods, and expectations. The same person can be extra-large in opinions, small in patience, and medium when it comes to saying thank you.

So what's the solution? Maybe there isn't one. The best we can do is stay true to our intent - do what's right, keep our conscience clear, and learn to smile through the noise. Because if we start living to please everyone, we'll end up pleasing no one - least of all ourselves.

And yes, before anyone raises an eyebrow - my Random Ramblings and Ruminations are meant for all, across age, gender, community, or nationality. Still, I doubt it'll please everyone at all times. That, my friend, would be against the very spirit of this piece